Intelligent Hands

why making is a skill for life

Charlotte Abrahams & Katy Bevan

*'Whoever wants to be a good philosopher
ought to know how to mend his shoes too.'*

Rudolf Steiner, *Handwork Indications*

QUICKTHORN

Cover image:
Cleo Mussi Mosaics
photo: Carmel King
www.carmelking.com

Published by Quickthorn
info@quickthornbooks.com
www.quickthornbooks.com
@quickthornbooks

Editor: Katy Bevan
Design and Typesetting: Chris J Bailey
Printed in the UK by Cambrian

Printed in the UK on uncoated FSC certified paper

MIX
Paper from
responsible sources
FSC® C004116

British Library Cataloguing in Publication Data
applied for
ISBN: 978-1-7393160-2-0

Contents

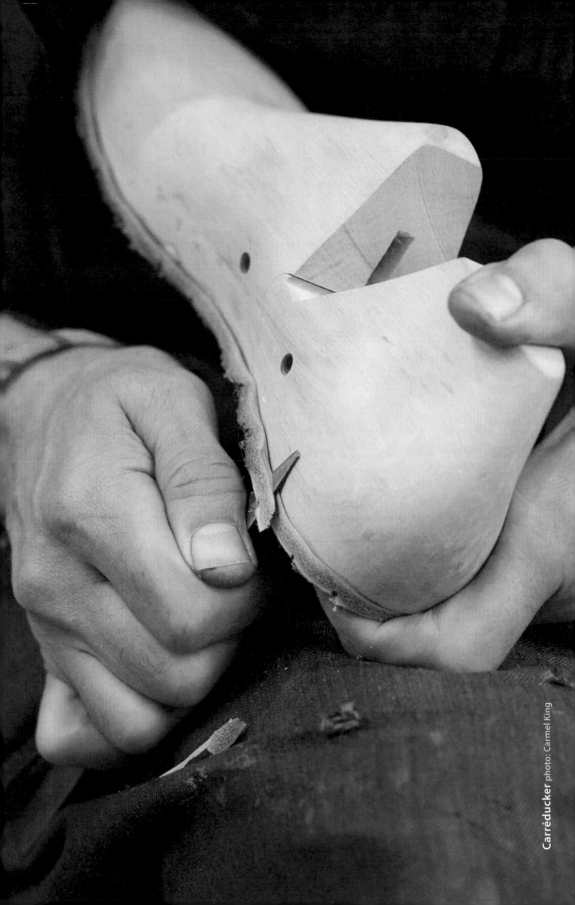

Foreword

photo: Amy Brathwaite

T he word craft can mean a lot of things nowadays, from making something at home on your kitchen table, to the skilled trades that sparked Britain's industrial revolution, to the high-end craftsmanship that the luxury goods sector capitalises on to sell us expensive cars and watches. There is a lot separating these types of activities, and often it is those working in craft that are the keenest to emphasise the differences. But there is also a lot uniting them.

I struggled with academic schooling when I was growing up and yet I have succeeded in my field, where my style of learning has been accommodated and my hands have proven my intelligence.

What I love about craft, and what this book captures so well here, is how it connects our often disconnected heads, hands and hearts in a way that few other activities can. In a world facing a mental health crisis, economic challenges and possible environmental collapse, I truly believe that craft is an important part of the solution, and that the first change is embracing our own shared humanity as makers.

Jay Blades MBE

Jay Blades MBE is presenter of The Repair Shop
and co-chair of Heritage Crafts

Introduction

'...we must come down to earth from the clouds where we live in vagueness and experience the most real thing there is: material.'

Anni Albers, *Work with Material, 1938*

Once the domain of well-to-do ladies, craft has gone mainstream, and from cross stitch to spoon carving, there is something for everyone. What is less well understood is that craft is good for us; not just for our general sense of wellbeing, but demonstrably good for our bodies and our brains, too.

Craft benefits our cognitive development, it improves our mental agility and it can also have a positive impact on our mental health.

Over 12 years ago I was working at the Crafts Council as their new Participation and Learning Manager. The Arts Council, from which a large majority of the funding came, had ordained that encouraging the public to participate in our activities was key to moving forward, and that the surest way to do this was through education and public events.

The idea of encouraging members of the public to engage with our activities was fairly new. Previously they had been invited to be observers, admirers and buyers of craft work at exhibitions and fairs, and while programmes aimed at the formal education of young people were lauded, it was never at the heart of what they did – more of an add on. At the root of the hesitation about education was a dichotomy between the aspiration towards excellence and a professional quality of work, and a horror of the amateur work of hobbyists who could give craft a bad name, with their crocheted toilet-roll holders and heavy-bottomed pottery. Surely it is hard enough for craftspeople to be taken seriously in the cultural world without being dragged down by amateurs? Attempts at collaborations with commercial knitting fairs and with the National Federation of Women's Institutes were met with the sort of derision about 'women of a certain age' and dilettante craftspeople that could only have been the result of a deep-seated insecurity.

It is generally acknowledged that craft is a good leisure pursuit, but, partly because of its domestic associations, craft has been downgraded in the unwritten international scale of what's 'worth doing'. It's true that

7

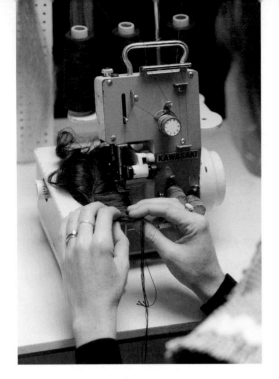

in the hierarchy of culture crafts are pretty low down, and quotidian textiles such as knitting and crochet are rock bottom. In schools, the Design and Technology curriculum has dropped any associations with craftiness, as has Art, so craft falls into a crack between the two. Neither artists nor designers want to be considered crafters, as this has a taint of the amateur hobbyist about it, and they are professionals, after all. What they do is an intellectual pursuit, a combination of aesthetics and concept that may happen to have an actual output.

It seems we have an image problem, so much so that some artists working in crafts do not want to be associated with magazines or organisations that might see them tarred with 'the C word'. I recently approached a sculptor working in weave for an interview, but when she discovered it was for Selvedge, a well-regarded textile magazine, she didn't want to know. I spoke to Grayson Perry,

pre-Turner Prize, when he was exhibiting his pots in a private art gallery in Savile Row, for *Ceramic Review* and he had no such problem embracing both worlds, but sadly he remains an exception. In his Reith Lecture series, Playing to the Gallery, Perry remarked that the art world was far more shocked by presenting pottery as art than by his crossdressing. Made between 2011 and 2020, Perry's Tomb of the Unknown Craftsman, at the British Museum, champions the nameless makers whose skills created some of our best-loved historical treasures.

Being thought of as a craftsperson means your work may command less in the art market, or indeed be excluded altogether – a familiar experience for most craftspeople. In what we would now call 'cultural capital', the work of an artisan is not considered as worthy as the output of an artist or academic, and this will be born out in the rewards they are offered in both financial

From left: **Making at The Posticherie; Kashket & Partners; Heidi Hockenjos; Chris Bramble Ceramics**

photos: Carmel King

and social terms. It is only in recent years that textiles and ceramics have entered the hallowed halls of the Tate Gallery, with recent shows about the work of Anni Albers and Magdalena Abakanowicz and the occasional piece of studio pottery. Parents aspire for their offspring the life and rewards of a professional, a lawyer or doctor with good career prospects, white collar, clean fingernails and a steady wage, so why would they want them to learn craft at school when they could be learning their times tables? This book argues that not only are the two not mutually exclusive, but that head and hand must beneficially co-exist. Indeed, in order to be successful at any role, from academic to surgeon, having learned to use one's hands at an early age will be advantageous, through developing dexterity of mind as well as hand.

What if we gave some recognition and status to those who do the practical jobs we don't want to think about, such as caring for the vulnerable while on the minimum wage and with poor job security? We question why an office job is considered superior to a trade, whether as a plumber or a potter. Somewhere along the line, the idea has taken hold that white-collar work is best and that working with our hands is only for people who can't use their heads.

In the following pages, we look at this phenomenon and at the historical precedents that led us here, and we will set out why hand skills are crucial in education and for lifelong learning. This is something we need to change; to revisit what we as a society choose to value – and why we need to make sure children are being taught these physical skills at an early age to make sure they are prepared for every eventuality.

There has been a lot of research into the importance of crafts for our wellbeing and

Turning Earth photo: Carmel King

development over the last 20 years, though much in such divergent sectors that they are rarely joined together, separated as they are into silos such as health, education, neurology and special needs education. Specialists in these sectors tend not to have exposure to each other, but once you start seeing the research more holistically, the picture becomes a lot clearer.

Through the three sections of this book – Mind and Body, Education and Learning, Wellbeing and Activism – we'll be looking at how physical labouring became separated from academic study; how movement is intelligent; how we became divorced from the materials that surround us, and the important role that crafts have to play in education as well as for our mental health – not just for the lower streams in schools, but for everyone. In short, we will reveal how making is good for you and gives you intelligent hands. **Katy Bevan**

The Nature of Gothic
by John Ruskin,
Kelmscott Press, 1890s.

Part One

Mind + Body

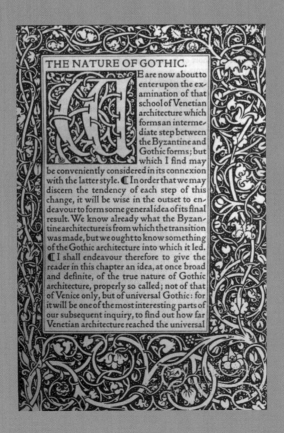

The thinking hand

'The hand is the window on to the mind.'

Immanuel Kant

It's obvious that we need our hands to feed information to our brains about the physical world, such as texture or heat, and our brains to tell our hands what to do. However, developments in neuroscience mean that we now know this is a two-way street; as information flows it changes the neural pathways and can even create new ones, while the brain is developing and giving the hands more things to do. Which came first is like the chicken and egg debate.

Tools and the word

When the first axe head was made, the range of things that could be killed, eaten, grown and built expanded hugely. Symmetrical, almond-shaped stone or flint heads are thought to have been the first prehistoric tools, which were named Acheulean after the place where ancient examples of these were found – Saint-Acheul, near Amiens in northern France.

Surprisingly sophisticated, these axes are often cited as being related to other sorts of articulation, something that was noted by Charles Darwin in 1871 in *The Descent of Man*. It is thought that speech in early mankind developed alongside toolmaking, as both these activities have been shown to occur in similar parts of the brain.[1] In support of this theory, more recent research by Natalie Uomini and Georg Meyer, at the University of Oxford, used the benefit of ultrasound to demonstrate that the same part of the brain is activated while cutting a stone axe head as is used in word generation. According to their research paper, 'This is consistent with a shared neural substrate for prehistoric stone toolmaking and language, and is compatible with language evolution theories that posit a co-evolution of language and manual praxis. In turn, our results support the hypothesis that aspects of language might have emerged as early as 1.75 million years ago, with the start of Acheulean technology.'[2]

Philosopher Friedrich Engels went further, he thought that working with the hands developed the brain, and thus 'labour created man himself.'[3]

The Casa Loredan, Venice,
John Ruskin, 1850
(Isabella Stewart Gardner Museum, Boston)

'First comes labour, after it, and then side by side with it, articulate speech – these were the two most essential stimuli under the influence of which the brain of the ape gradually changed into that of man, which for all its similarity to the former is far larger and more perfect. Hand in hand with the development of the brain went the development of its most immediate instruments – the sense organs. Just as the gradual development of speech is inevitably accompanied by a corresponding refinement of the organ of hearing, so the development of the brain as a whole is accompanied by a refinement of all the senses.'

Frank Wilson talks about the articulate hand in his book *The Hand*, pointing out the link

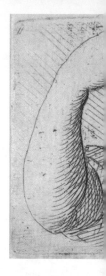

**Hands and arms, print,
Wenceslaus Hollar,**
1644–52
(Metropolitan Museum of Art)

between the loss of words and the loss of movement in those who have suffered a brain injury or stroke. Those who have aphasia – which is when a person has lost the ability to speak or to say certain things, perhaps because of a stroke – would have the same difficulty if they were using sign language. It is not a damage to the voice of the brain, but of the language-processing part of the cerebral cortex.

Haptics

Remember the TV ad for a German car, where men in lab coats were experimenting with a different sound and feel of a car door closing, with satisfying feedback? That's haptics in a nutshell, and there's a lot of research being done in this area, not least in the development of robotics and touch technology. Research has shown that it's not just what the hand is doing, but the order and sequencing that gives feedback to the brain. Some of this also shows that kinaesthetic learning (a tacit style of learning) promotes greater understanding.

Ceramics designer and teacher Camilla Groth[4] analysed craft thinking as embodied cognition, where the body is used as a knowledge provider. She noted the importance of the emotions and feelings of the maker when interacting with and evaluating materials: 'Sensory experiences are keys to sense-making in material manipulation. What is seen by the eye

is confirmed by touch, and through our hands we are able to interact with and test the material, learning by doing and acting; thus we also shape our minds and affect our future actions with similar or new materials.'

She also notes how this affects the nature of the final objects created, which are usually for a person to use, and that items that are designed without thought to the material they are made from will have a poorer outcome: 'As we as human beings continue to be physical, we will always have physical needs, and part of the designer's or craft practitioner's task will still be to improve and develop material objects for physical use.'

In his praise of the gothic style, nineteenth-century English art historian John Ruskin[5] notes the quality of a work, including any mistakes, as part of its value and goes on to describe the nature of the worker to be observed in their work, including being 'savage' or rude and having a love of nature.

If it's about creativity and understanding as well as dexterity, do you have to be a genius to begin with? Susan Magsamen and Ivy Ross, the authors of the book *Your Brain on Art*, say: 'Learning is, from a neurobiological

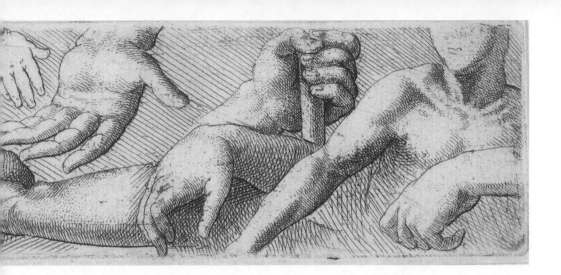

perspective, a dynamic process driven by experiences that change your brain in enduring ways. When your brain is learning, it's making and shifting synapses to sculpt new circuits that weren't there before and that encode memory. Salient experiences enhance synaptic plasticity...'[6]

So it's not that people with larger brains make better artists or musicians, but that practising art made their brains bigger; creative making shapes the brain and contributes to cognitive development.

Tacit knowledge

Just like learning to ride a bike, we learn a new skill by first witnessing a demonstration or reading about it, then we have a go – with much concentration and occasional mishaps. Eventually, practice means that we can ride along without giving it any thought, so it becomes automatic, or tacit. However, trying to pass on tacit knowledge is difficult, so the next person will also have to watch and try for themselves.

Neurophysiologist Nikolai Bernstein's[7] work on motor learning and dexterity back in the 1930s suggested that physically learning was a way of developing a skill. His theories were based on the concept of intentional movements, rather than the prevalent ideas of his contemporary, Ivan Pávlov – he of the salivating dog story – who preferred the idea of reflexive action. This is important because the action is performed with a notion of how it will affect the future and is therefore deliberate and thoughtful; that is, it is intelligent movement. How the ability to perform these motor movements can be affected by development is key.

Muscle memory exists and learning in a real-world environment can have a lasting effect. So, just like riding that bike, it becomes tacit knowledge. Eventually, practice means that we can execute an action without giving it any thought, and so it has become ingrained.

It's hard to teach someone something that you can do without thinking about it, even harder to learn something just from watching. In her paper 'The New Journeyman', Nicola Wood[8] proposed the idea of an expert learner who can ask relevant questions that elicit helpful responses from the teacher. The conversation between the two transmits the knowledge in a useful way so we can join in.

story
First class

George was an academic boy. A clean sweep of top grades at GCSE led to the same again at A level, then a First in PPE (Philosophy, Politics & Economics) from the University of Exeter. The expectation from teachers, parents, friends — and himself, too — was that he would work with his head rather than his hands. Then, aged 26, he decided a change was needed. This is his story.

My dad is very keen on DIY and I remember as a child being amazed at the things he could make. It seemed like magic the way that old, wonky bits of the house could be pulled down and put right with two hands, a few tools and some head scratching. That feeling has stayed with me and it's one of the things I like most about the work I do now as a trainee carpenter. At the end of my working day there is some tangible thing standing where before there was nothing – a new wall, a balcony, a roof.

Working with my hands is not something that I ever thought I would do. I went to a grammar school that valued academic ability over pretty much anything else. Everyone around me was extremely high-achieving and we had assemblies on topics such as 'getting one per cent better every day'. Manual work was a last resort, not discussed unless everything else went wrong.

When it came to higher education it was never a question of if we'd like to go to university or do something else, it was only which university we wanted to study at. There was an unspoken assumption that if you were able to get the academic grades to go to university, then that's what you would do. And so I did.

I studied PPE at Exeter for four years. The environment was the same as it had been at school, only this time the assumptions were about jobs rather than further study. We had talks from accountancy firms, law firms, banks, the civil service and consumer goods companies. I really felt at the time that the only option for 'success' was to get the kind of job that required a suit and an office. I applied for a few things, mostly unpaid internships, going

George Siddons

photo: Angel-Emerald Lish

through rounds of online interviews and psychometric testing without much success. There was one question on the application forms that I always struggled with, which was: 'Tell us why you want to work in marketing/PR/finance/the civil service?'. Whatever the job was, this question always stumped me because I could never think of a single reason why I did, beyond the fact that these were the kind of jobs you were supposed to apply for when you'd done a degree like mine. I never got anywhere with those applications, probably because it was obvious on every form that I'd fudged the answer to that crucial question.

After university I spent a few years travelling and drifting through jobs that were easy to pick up and put down, always with this growing feeling that I wished I'd learned some useful skill. Then, in the summer of 2022, I decided to apply for a part-time City & Guilds Site Carpentry course at my local college. There was an informal interview on the open day and the first question that the tutor asked me was, 'Why do you want to do Site Carpentry?' Easy question: I wanted to make things, I wanted to fix things, I wanted to have the skills I needed to build my own house, and

I wanted to have a job that contributed something tangible and useful to the world. I started the course in September and found a job working on site the same week.

The first job I did on site alone was to plasterboard both sides of an internal wall. It's a pretty straightforward task for a chippy but I had never done any plasterboarding before and I was winging it, to be honest. The first few panels I put in took me ages. There were gaps all over the place, crooked bits and more than one rough edge. But slowly, with each panel that I cut, the edges got straighter and smoother, and the gaps got smaller. I started to notice mistakes before I made them and, with some tips from the more experienced guys on site, I started to work a bit faster. After a couple of days, it was finished. I stood back and looked over my work. It was okay. I gave it a little nod of approval and packed up my tools with a feeling I'd never really had from my studies or previous jobs; a feeling of satisfaction at a job well done. I had made something.

And that feeling has been repeated many times since. Site carpentry is hard, physical work and I'm out in the elements all day, but I'm finally doing a job that I find fulfilling.

Rooksmoor Press photo: Carmel King

Mind vs body

It seems obvious that the mind tells the body what to do and the brain gets its information from the body, the two working in unison, so how is it that the mind and body came to be divided in our culture? Think about the academic, or egg head, the stereotypical scientist with a brain the size of a planet compared with the tabloid image of a footballer with lightning feet and no sense. Here's a pocket history of the subject – and we need to go back a bit.

Cogito ergo sum

René Descartes (1596–1650), he of 'I think therefore I am' fame, was all about the mind being more important that the body; theology over form, if you like. In his world view, perceptions through the senses of the real world were not to be trusted; the thoughts of the head, even dreams, were more reliable. This dualism put mind and body up against each other. Thus Cartesian Dualism – Cartesius just means Descartes in Latin – was born and the whole debate about mind versus body began.

During the so-called Age of Enlightenment, Immanuel Kant (1724–1804) wrote a lot of admirable things about democracy and international cooperation, but his *Critique of Pure Reason* expounded the total authority of human reason and the intellect over the physical world, making the dualism even more extreme. He divided the human experience into the inner and outer spheres, so 'the hand is the visible part of the brain'. However, his idea was that we can only experience the world through the prism of the mind, therefore we can never really be sure that it exists.

The senses

How we experience sensory perception has developed into a whole field of inquiry. Suffice to say, there has been some disagreement about how and what information we receive

19

from our senses, such as touch and sight. For many in the mainstream, the conclusion of all this thinking has been that the brain is good and senses that feed the information are, by their nature, unreliable.

Move up to the twenty-first century and we now have the development of theories of embodied cognition that acknowledge that thinking can come from somewhere other than the brain. Professor Bill Lucas[9] has spoken about Descartes and the idea that the mind and body are separate: 'The tragedy of the English Baccalaureate goes back to this, and they are both wrong,' he said. 'The theory of embodied cognition is the missing link in education: numeracy, literacy, "manipulate"; the words haven't caught up.'

Lucas and his team's argument is that hands-on learning should be a normal element in schools and their research has been well received as a vocational pedagogy by City & Guilds, for example. He says, 'Craft is a tool for creativity, and that creative thinking has the power to relieve boredom and make life more enjoyable.' To that end, Lucas writes about creative learning: not just acquiring knowledge and skills, but also 'capabilities' that will be useful throughout later life, such as creativity, self-perception and resilience.

Design vs craft

Those who work in design do not like to be tarred with the brush of craft. The schools and colleges that held the title of 'design' and 'craft' have been renamed to lose any taint of practicality. Design has the image of being modern and professional, so that it has become a clean, intellectual pursuit. Camilla Groth at the University of South-Eastern Norway has been doing research into the theory of embodied cognition,[10] where the physical world influences the mind. Design thinking is generally presented as an intellectual planning activity, raising design above the stigma associated with physical labour. 'This view, although plausible in the way it portrays the designer as a thinker, separates designing and making into two entities, leaving making behind as merely part of the implementation phase,' she states. Making or crafting the design idea is thus situated at the end of the design process, perhaps by someone else, seemingly not requiring intellectual activity.

The results of Groth's study suggest that the physical making and crafting of a design involves the embodied mind. She further claims that the act of thinking or planning a design relies on accumulated embodied knowledge. Groth shows what we already know – that it makes sense that a designer would need to understand the properties of the material they are designing for, its strength and elasticity, for example. Through our physical experiences of the material world, we create mental images that we rely on in the design process, thus the body provides information also in the planning phase of designing, even before material manipulation. Therefore, the body is a crucial contributor to knowledge.

Creative workshop photo: courtesy of The Creative Dimension Trust

story
The Creative Dimension Trust

When Penny Bendall said she was going to art college rather than university, her decision was met by some teachers and peers with sceptical silence. She went ahead undaunted and a hugely successful career as a ceramics conservator followed – she holds a Royal Warrant and has worked with institutions such as The Fitzwilliam Museum, in Cambridge, and Sir John Soane's Museum, in London, as well as the auction houses Christie's and Sotheby's. She is also a Fellow of the International Institute for Conservation of Historic and Artistic Works to boot.

However, that early reaction to her decision left its mark; 'I've always had a real thing about the academic snobbery around working with your hands,' she says. That 'thing' is the motivation behind The Creative Dimension Trust (TCDT), the charity she founded in 2015 to help young people develop fine hand skills as a way of inspiring future careers. 'I was extremely lucky,' Penny says, explaining how the Trust came about. 'I was working on a collection of ceramics belonging to an influential family and we got talking. I said that there was nowhere in the UK where teenagers had the chance to learn craft skills at the highest level, using the best materials. They asked me what I wanted to do about it and I said I'd like the chance to put some workshops together to see if the kids responded. They gave me some money and told me to do a pilot.'

The money funded two week-long workshops for 24 teenagers. Half of them studied with gilders from the Royal Collection Trust and the rest learned marquetry techniques with the man responsible for all the marquetry work at Wells Cathedral. The teenagers' response

21

was to work extremely hard and, by the end of the week, they had produced fabulous, quality pieces under the guidance of these master craftspeople. Penny was bowled over and The Creative Dimension Trust was born.

Today, those two workshops have swelled to 40 and there is a waiting list of 14–19-year-olds keen to give up their free time to learn skills ranging from embroidery to sign writing on skateboards, via plaster carving and chair-making. The workshops are free and take place in the school holidays, and 80 per cent of the students come from areas of social or economic deprivation. As with those early pilots, the teachers are global specialists and the students are given the finest materials and tools to work with. 'A lot of schools don't have the resources to provide good materials,' says Penny. 'If you don't have good materials, your ability to progress will be limited. We give our students the best and in return we expect them to do their best with them. The idea that it doesn't matter whether the finished product is good or bad is nonsense. It does matter.'

A belief in excellence and professionalism lies at the heart of TCDT's ethos. Their intention is not to give students a nice hobby but to show them that they can make a viable profession out of working with their hands. Alongside the technical skills, they are taught about how to make things that people want to buy, about the tendering process, and even about the importance of good time-keeping. By way of encouragement, they are awarded a grade (working towards, pass, merit or distinction) at the end of their training and the chance to exhibit their work in an annual installation designed by set designer, curator and TCDT trustee Simon Costin in the window of upmarket department store Fortnum & Mason, in central London.

Many of the students lucky enough to gain a place on one of the workshops do go on to work in the craft industry, but TCDT's remit is broader than that. Their workshops help the teenagers develop

Creative workshop

photos courtesy of The Creative Dimension Trust

Students trying out stone carving

visual sensitivity, to think in three dimensions, and to problem solve – transferrable skills that have taken alumni into fields as diverse as architecture, science and medicine. As the Head of Science at one of the participating schools in London commented on the charity's blog, 'When students take part in workshops at TCDT, I have seen for myself... they're paying attention to detail, they're having to work accurately, they're having to measure. These are all transferable skills, skills they will use again in the future.' Beyond that there are many general life benefits too, such as improved concentration, more self-confidence and higher self-esteem.

'The workshops are designed so that at the end of the week all the students have got something they've made,' explains Penny. 'We've begun to keep some of the things to sell at an event we hold at the end of the summer workshops. The money goes to help other kids have the same opportunity. That makes the students really proud.'

Jay

Jay Patel took part in a week-long stone carving workshop run by The Creative Dimension Trust when he was 17. He believes that this chance encounter changed the course of his life. This is his story:

Jay Patel designing at The Creative Dimension Trust

I was at college studying for my A levels and one day an email arrived in my inbox from the Art and Design tutor about a stone masonry workshop being run over the summer holidays by The Creative Dimension Trust. I had never heard of them, and I didn't know anything about stone carving, but I thought, why not? It was free and I liked working with my hands. There were 14 of us from all over London, and we were taught by the renowned stone carver Nancy Peskett. The project for the week was to make an archway.

Creative workshops

We made a bird bath first to learn the basics, then we each worked on our own stone for the arch.

As soon as I walked into the workshop I thought, 'Wow! There's this whole world of stone masonry that I didn't even know existed'. I was thinking about being an architect, and doing the course both reinforced that idea and made me question whether it was the right route for me after all. I noticed that what I was carving was very architectural, but I found the physical process of shaping the stone really rewarding because I could literally feel the progress I was making. You don't get that working on a computer screen.

I went back to college and finished my A levels but I kept in touch with TCDT, and the following summer I went along to an installation being organised by Grimshaw Architects that the trust was helping with. While we were there, a group of us were invited for a tour of the Grimshaw offices. I was still thinking about architecture as a career but I'd never seen how architects worked, or met one in person, so I went along. It was fantastic, with all these models on display! I knew immediately that this was what I wanted to do. My enthusiasm obviously showed because I was offered a week's work experience. Four years on, I am a Part 1 Architectural Assistant and well on my way to becoming fully qualified.

That would never have happened had I not stumbled across TCDT. Besides meeting Grimshaw Architects (and there's no way on earth I would have done that without the Trust), I have learned to make things. I have carved stone, I have done etching and printmaking and, most recently, I worked with architectural gilders to restore the torches that sit either side of the main entrance to Fortnum & Mason on Piccadilly. Those making experiences have allowed me to understand the big wide world of arts and crafts that is so often overlooked in the academically inclined society we live in. I now really value each block of stone I specify because I know that someone had to carve it, and I know how much skill that requires.

photos: courtesy of The Creative Dimension Trust

Good work

The snobbery about amateur craft negates the value of the making process and the learning involved. C. S. Lewis wrote an essay about the distinction between good work and *Good Works*[11] – acts that are considered to be good, or worthy, but also from the perspective of their quality. In it he declares, 'Good works are chiefly alms-giving or "helping" in the parish. They are quite separate from one's "work". And good works need not be good work, as anyone can see by inspecting some of the objects made to be sold at bazaars for charitable purposes.'

Lewis goes on to talk about built-in obsolescence and the dearth of the well-made, where 'bad work' is desirable for business as it will necessitate further purchases, and that many people are necessarily in jobs making things of poor quality to keep the wheels of industry turning: 'We shall try, if we get the chance, to earn our living by doing well what would be worth doing even if we had not our living to earn.' This was essentially Richard Sennett's argument in his work *The Craftsman*. But who are the gatekeepers that decide what quality looks like?

The Master's Touch[12] by Alberto Cavalli was launched at Homo Faber in 2018, a new biennial for craft in Venice. It considers the criteria by which excellence can be measured, including local traditions from particular regions, as well as skills. Cavalli has isolated eleven terms that can be used to judge whether a work is 'good'. These are divided into criteria around locality, such as territory and tradition; the skill of the maker is appraised by their competence,

creativity, training, interpretation, talent; and the thing itself through the lens of craftsmanship, innovation, originality and authenticity.

The motivation behind this is laudable – to find a common language across diverse regions and countries in order to enable a replicable standard for artisanship. To have the title of Master of Craft – *Mestieri d'Arte* or, as the Japanese say, Living Treasures – is to elevate the status of craftspeople and would go some way towards raising the appreciation of crafts, while also raising its cultural value.

Cynically, you might think that this has been funded in part by the business of luxury brands who would like to maintain the cachet of labels such as 'Made in Italy' – and you would be right. However, where this feeds back into better recognition and conditions for the makers and the sustainability of the industry, it must be a good thing. The Homo Faber project is funded by the Michelangelo Foundation for Creativity and Craftsmanship, itself founded by Franco Cologni, a director of the watchmakers Cartier International, and Johann Rupert, a South African businessman. Cologni is also the founder of Fondazione Cologni dei Mestieri d'Arte, which promotes the life and work of artisans. Germany has introduced the Meisterpflicht, or master craftsperson certificate, saying only people with the requisite experience, generally five years, can set up a crafts business.

The United Nations Educational, Scientific and Cultural Organization (UNESCO) is concerned to safeguard intangible cultural heritage (ICH), including traditional craftsmanship such as drystone walling in Croatia or the ancient tradition of wooden architecture in China. In 2003, a UNESCO convention was created and established in international law. It has since been adopted by 178 countries to make ICH part of their cultural policy. The UK has yet to sign up to this convention, something that Heritage Crafts is campaigning for, which would ensure that traditional skills in the UK are protected alongside the art of Shital Pati weaving from Sylhet, in eastern Bangladesh; Tinian marble-carving from Greece; or a rare form of needle lace-making from Alençon in Normandy, France.

So there are criteria for judging whether work is good, but what of the so-so output of workshops where people are enjoying learning? Do we measure the other benefits that may come from the production of a warm blanket for charity, or the joy of being part of a common endeavour? This is also true in schools, where the non-cognitive skills are not measured for league tables. These are the social and emotional 'soft' skills that help people to navigate relationships and their place in the world, and invaluable in the workplace.

story
yard:ARTspace

Artist Sue Brown uses intaglio printmaking to tell stories and her work is regularly exhibited in museums and galleries across the UK. She is also the director of the yard:ARTspace in Cheltenham and the author of the step-by-step guide *Paper Lithography* (The Crowood Press). When the Covid-19 pandemic changed everyone's lives overnight, she found herself feeling restless and uninspired. Her solution was to launch a community making project called Same Sea, Different Boat. This is her story.

Not long into the first lockdown in spring 2020, I realised that the artists who used to come to my courses and workshops at the yard:ARTspace were feeling isolated, so I started posting Sunday art prompts on my Instagram feed. I didn't want to teach online, but I did do one Zoom meeting to show them how to make a collagraph plate at home and suggested that if local artists dropped their plates through my door on their daily walk, I could ink them up and drop them back.

It was a success and the comments on my Instagram page were grateful, but by the middle of May I sensed that the enthusiasm of the students had waned. Everyone was losing their creative energy, me included. I'm the kind of artist who needs a deadline, so with all this time on my hands, I found I couldn't make my own work. And I couldn't just sit about doing nothing either. So, I thought, what if I expand the plates-through-the-door trial with the aim of creating a community patchwork quilt?

I'm not a textile artist, I'm a printmaker, but I dabble with textiles and a quilt felt right for this project. Quilts have a tradition of communal making, they hold memories, and they speak of comfort. You can hang a quilt on the wall, but really you just want to wrap yourself up in it.

I made a page on my website explaining the idea. It was simple; people were invited to post me a 10 × 10cm (4 × 4in) drawing or collagraph plate (I provided step-by-step instructions) describing

**Same Sea,
Different Boat**

photo: courtesy of Sue Brown

their experience of lockdown, along with a stamped addressed envelope. I would then ink up the plate, print it on a fabric square and send it back to be stitched or embellished in some way. The finished squares would then be returned to me to be sewn together into a patchwork quilt. I called the project Same Sea, Different Boat because that's how the pandemic felt – the entire world was going through the same thing but all of us were experiencing it in very different ways.

I asked a couple of fellow creatives and workshop providers, Louise Asher at Hope & Elvis, Nottingham, and Liske Johnson at Littleheath Barn Studios, Bromsgrove, to help spread the word. Louise put it on her Instagram, I did the same, and then things got really silly... By the end of the month over 200 collagraph plates had landed on my door mat, and there were stitched squares too. The postman wondered what was going on.

Squares came from all over the world and from all kinds of people. The first to arrive was a simply drawn dog with staring eyes. I printed it and sent it back, then when it returned it had been given the most beautifully embroidered collar. Textile artists Alice Fox and Cas Holmes sent things, and we had three plates from a non-verbal young man in America. There are a whole series of squares by children from a local primary school, too – I'd met them in a park and bellowed instructions on how to make a collagraph across the social distance. A few squares were anonymous, many were accompanied by letters thanking us for doing the project and others came with stories. There were quirky ones like the drawing of a set of teeth from someone who had suffered from terrible toothache and hadn't been able to see a dentist. And there were ones that moved me to tears – a mother's drawing of her nurse daughter behind a face mask, and a widow's memorial square to her husband. My eldest son sent me a square with an image from the film Harvey, because it was a memory from Christmas when he was a child and he was missing family Christmases. My husband recreated the allotment and nearly burst a vein trying to do a French knot.

Same Sea, Different Boat

photo: courtesy of Sue Brown

I made a fish and a series of 19 Covid corvids – I'm fascinated by all things ornithological and once I started, I couldn't stop.

By June we had almost 400 squares. It was clear that we'd be making a very large quilt. My friend, textile and quilt artist Catherine Kingzett, came to help us sew the squares onto panels. There was no curation, we just divided the squares between the four of us and we included everything we'd been sent.

Looking at those first four finished panels was a revelation. I think if I over-analyse it, it will take away the magic, but there was something very levelling about the process of turning these squares into a patchwork. It probably helped that all the squares were the same size and that I printed everything in Prussian blue (I made it clear that I would do that right from the start so people didn't ask to have theirs in green or pink), but you simply couldn't tell which had been made by experienced printers or quilters and which were by people doing this for the first time.

And they didn't – still don't – scream hopelessness. I thought that lots of squares would be negative or complaining and all of them would be filled with a massive sense of anxiety. But it was quite the opposite – each square is a celebration of creativity in a time of unprecedented crisis. I wonder whether that was about the process of making something with beautiful things, because people did use beautiful things to make their squares.

By the end of 2022 we had over 600 squares sewed into seven panels (there were some spaces on number seven) and the project had also been exhibited in various museums and galleries around the UK. It was exciting to see the work on show, but public exhibitions were never the intention. For me as an artist, it's aways about the doing rather than the finished piece, and that was even more true with this project. The making of it joined everyone who took part together with a single, shared purpose, and that made us feel less isolated. We were featured on Woman's Hour on BBC Radio 4 in August 2020 and the interviewer just couldn't understand the idea that these squares were sent in, then returned to the maker, then sent back to me again. But that was the point – it was a conversation. Isn't that what a community project should be?

Silence, organzine silk, Ariane
Fourquier, RCA, 2021

photo: courtesy of Ariane Fourquier

Risk

Danger is something that we have to learn
to live with; from pandemics to the existential
threat of climate change that bring with them
an increasing risk of unemployment, sickness
or death. It is this kind of uncertainty that we
have had to adjust to in recent years.

Connectivity and computers enable many of us
to work from home while surrounded by opaque
technology. It's easy to see how this new way of
working is reliant on computers and gadgets
that most of us cannot comprehend the insides
of. It used to be that you could fix a phone with

a screwdriver, but now we throw away and buy
new when things become broken or out of
date. So we are again being alienated from the
things that we rely on to keep us connected.
No wonder there is an increased appetite for
the great outdoors, making and the tangible.

Our ability to adapt to new situations without
undue anxiety and to take risks accordingly is a
learned skill. Those who have had the benefit of
learning in the outdoors, perhaps in uncertain
weather, walking and orienteering, cooking on
wood fires, will be more adaptable and less

shaken when events threaten to destabilise our situation. They may feel more in control of their environment, less frightened by sudden events.

Similarly, working with our hands introduces an element of risk, encouraging choices and decision making. Working with clay, fire or sharp tools demands concentration and an element of jeopardy. Even decisions about design, colour or texture demand a certain level of risk-taking: will it look okay, what if it doesn't work? This gives the maker an improved confidence to innovate and a sense of agency or control over their environment and greater resilience to withstand external pressures.

Making encourages people with low confidence to begin to make decisions and take risks. Even small choices, such as what colour or pattern to use, can be a start. And, unlike in life, if you make a mistake in your knitting, say, it's easy to unravel, or you could decide to live with your mistake. Either way, it's a great life lesson.

Royal College of Art student Ariane Fourquier is a researcher and weaver creating woven designs for trauma therapy purposes. Her designs contain deliberate errors, of which she says: 'These mistakes represent scars and the idea that the memory of a trauma will persist, but that it is possible to live with it.'

Being more adaptable to change increases resilience and the ability to deal with all the stuff that life throws at us. Safe risk-taking is a tool for learning that benefits everyone.

Silence, organzine silk, Ariane Fourquier, RCA, 2021

photo: courtesy of Ariane Fourquier

Part Two

Education + Learning

Progressive education

'We need to radically rethink our view of intelligence...'

Sir Ken Robinson

There are hundreds of educational theories and approaches to creative education, with changes made over the years through the work of inspired individuals. We will look at only a few here that have relevance, so it's a whirlwind tour, but you'll get the gist of it. If you have studied the theory of education, look away now.

Johann Heinrich Pestalozzi (1746–1827)

Pestalozzi wanted education for all, regardless of their social status. A Swiss educational reformer – he's the one who came up with the phrase 'head, heart and hand', which you'll have heard in other contexts. Albert Einstein went to a school that followed his ideas, the Old Cantonal School Aarau, in Switzerland. It had an emphasis on learning through the senses, including touch, sight and visualisation, which Einstein later claimed helped him to visualise problems through what he called 'thought experiments'. Einstein said of his education at Aarau, 'When compared to six years' schooling at a German authoritarian

gymnasium, it made me clearly realise how much superior an education based on free action and personal responsibility is to one relying on outward authority.'[1]

Friedrich Froebel (1782–1852)

A student of Pestalozzi, Froebel believed that a child is born to be active and that their education should be personally tailored. It was he who founded the concept of the kindergarten, and his educational theories include self-directed play and the importance of movement, suggesting outdoor play and finger games. Froebel said that 'the activity of the child should be the agency by which its early education should be promoted.'

Wilhelm von Humboldt (1767–1835)

Von Humboldt thought that all people would benefit from a rounded cultural education, regardless of what they went on to do in life, as it would create fully rounded citizens. He believed in education for its own sake, and the motto 'Knowledge is power and education is liberty' is attributed to him. Believing that everyone is an individual and we are all citizens of the world, he extended

Forest School
prospectus c.1938

FOREST SCHOOL
WHITWELL   REEPHAM   NORFOLK

core education ideas to include languages, critical studies and culture.

Humboldt's ideas formed the basis of the Prussian education model until the 1930s, and he is considered to be the father of the modern university system, having founded Berlin University, now Humboldt University, where, perhaps not coincidentally, Einstein also studied.

Folk schools

This concept originally came from the Danish writer, philosopher and Lutheran pastor N. F. S. Grundtvig (1783–1872), who advocated 'schools for life', where students are prepared for active citizenship. An alternative to university, hands-on work was emphasised along with freedom of thought,

the theory being that removing the pressure of grades and exams allows individuals the freedom to learn and think around subject themes. Originally rural schools for the children of farmers, folk schools went on to be adult education colleges promoting lifelong learning. The premise took off in Denmark, where there were 83 schools by 1914. Today there are around 400 folk schools operating in Scandinavian countries, northern Europe and the US.

There are 74 folk high schools in Finland alone, and 81 campuses all around the country. By any standards, Finland's education system is a success story; according to their PISA score (the Programme for International Student Assessment), which assesses children at

15 years old, students in Finland scored higher than the OECD average in reading, mathematics and science.[2] How they have managed this may have some reflection on the country's history of education and the folk school tradition.

The Finnish curriculum includes transferable skills – what they call transversal competencies – including life skills. Crafts, or *käsityö*, became compulsory in 1866, in a bid to develop aesthetic, technical and psycho-motor skills. Each year is based around a common theme, with each subject area looking at different aspects. This means teaching is not only cross-curricular but also involves vertical age groups working and learning together. Feedback to students, parents and carers is regularly held as a discussion, rather than according to grades. There is also an element of self and peer appraisal, so it is much more like an enlightened workplace than the system we know in the UK. Finland is using a holistic approach, with cooperation rather than competition being the norm, although university entrance is still based on an end-of-school exam.

In 2014 a new craft curriculum was introduced, including a concept of multi-materiality, which caused much discussion. The idea was to mix up the hard and soft crafts of textiles and woodwork, for instance, to confound the gender silos that have historically followed. However, despite being

Normal class at the free sloyd school, *Popular Science Monthly*, New York, 1890.

an admirable idea it has proved more difficult to put into practice.

Sloyd, or *slöjd*

This approach was developed by Uno Cygnaeus in Finland in the mid-1850s, based on the ideas of Froebel and Pestalozzi. Sloyd, also known as Educational Sloyd, is a form of pedagogical craft – that is, the desired outcome is the development of the child rather than anything they might make.

As a system of educational handwork its purpose is not to turn out carpenters, but 'to develop the mental, moral and physical powers of children…'

Otto Salomon (1849–1907) took these ideas to Sweden and refined the concept, with woodwork becoming one of the foremost crafts featured. Private sloyd schools were funded by the state 'for the purpose of developing skilled workers and promoting

the reinstatement of values of good citizenship'.[3] Salomon was keen to stress that sloyd should not be confused with the skilled work of the professional artisan: 'Educational *slöjd* differs from so-called practical *slöjd*, in as much as in the latter, importance is attached to the work; in the former, on the contrary, it is to the worker. It cultivates manual dexterity, self-reliance, accuracy, carefulness, patience, perseverance and especially does it train the faculty of attention and develop the powers of concentration.'

The sloyd theory was that people should be allowed to learn with their own hands and from their own mistakes, and teachers were discouraged from interfering too much. It was said that 'the teacher teaches best who teaches least', and that the teacher should never touch what a student was working on. 'The teacher's art in educational slöjd consists essentially in being as passive and unobtrusive as possible, while the pupil is actively exercising both head and hand. Only in this way can the feeling of self-reliance arise and gain strength... He must work and think about his work – a sloyder cannot be an Automaton. Experience clearly indicates that adults generally are too cautious in their work, and desire more help from the teacher than children do, and certainly far more than is good for them.'[4]

The aim was 'To utilise... the educative force which lies in rightly directed bodily labour, as a means of developing in the pupil physical and mental powers which will be a sure and evident gain to them for life.'[5] (Read more about sloyd on page 133.)

The English answer to sloyd came from the City & Guilds woodwork courses, which followed a similar system of steps to learn basic joints and techniques in joinery, with a few additions, such as an emphasis on drawing skills and a vocational outcome.[6]

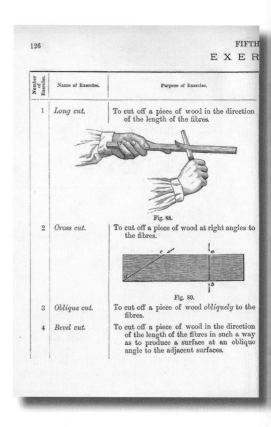

Woodwork exercise
from *The Teacher's Hand-book of Slöjd*,
Otto Salomon, 1892

The City & Guilds of London Institute (CGLI) was founded in 1878 when 16 trade guilds, or livery companies, joined with the City of London Corporation to support training for workers in the Industrial Revolution. Livery guilds traditionally managed the standards for each trade, such as the Clothworkers or Pewterers.

John Dewey (1859–1952)

A philosopher and a pragmatist whose progressive educational ideas included a hands-on approach, learning by doing. (He's nothing to do with the Dewey Decimal Classification system in libraries, that was Melvil Dewey and another story completely.) John Dewey developed the concept of Instrumentalism, where knowledge is not an absolute that can be learned by rote; instead, pupils must interact and learn from their ever-changing environment and thereby are empowered to interact with society.

Dewey wrote about democracy as social intelligence and vocational, purposeful learning having a moral worth.[7] Where school studies may remain abstract ideas, he believed that 'What is learned and employed in an occupation having an aim and involving cooperation with others is moral knowledge, whether consciously so regarded or not. For it builds up a social interest and confers the intelligence needed to make that interest effective in practice.' His vision for education was one where the school taught the whole citizen and included

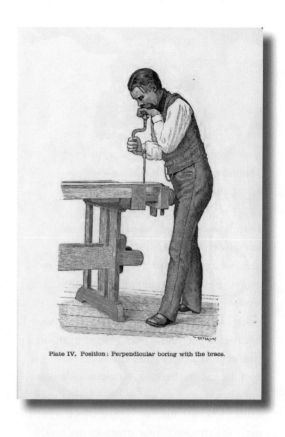

Plate IV. Position: Perpendicular boring with the brace.

**Perpendicular boring
with the brace**
from *The Teacher's
Hand-book of Slöjd*,
Otto Salomon, 1892

'...activities or occupations which have a social aim and utilise the materials of typical social situations.'

Dewey recognised the dualism between knowledge as an absolute to be learned and learning as an ongoing experience, as something between the intellect and emotions. He also recognised the class distinctions: 'Socially, it reflects a division between those who are controlled by direct concern with things and those who are free to cultivate themselves.'[8] Dewey's ideas on educational and social reorganisation were quite radical in his day, as perhaps they still are. He believed in teaching socially moral participation in all classes in order to promote democracy. 'It is accordingly an encouragement to those believing in a better order to undertake the promotion of a vocational education which does not subject youth to the demands and standards of the present system, but which utilise its scientific and social factors to develop a courageous intelligence, and to make intelligence practical and executive.'

Jean Piaget (1896–1980)

As part of his work as a psychologist, Piaget developed his theory about cognitive development while observing children take intelligence tests. He noticed that children gave wrong answers at different ages and he identified four distinct stages: Sensorimotor stage, birth to 2 years; Preoperational stage, 2 to 7 years; Concrete operational stage, 7 to 11 years; Formal operational stage, ages 12 and up. Piaget promoted learning from the experience of an object itself. His ideas fed into the Plowden Report on primary school education in 1967, which influenced educational policy from the late 1960s and proposed less reliance on IQ testing and more creativity in the classroom.

The most important takeaway from Piagetian theory is that he recognised that children didn't have less intelligence than adults, just a different quality of intelligence.

Steiner-Waldorf

In 1919 Rudolf Steiner (1861–1925) was commissioned by industrialist Emil Molt of the Waldorf Astoria company to create a school and a curriculum for workers' children at their factory in Stuttgart (hence the Steiner-Waldorf name). Steiner developed a theory of *anthroposophy* – from the Greek for human and wisdom – which combined his spiritual beliefs with physical reality. For him, education involved the alignment of the body and mind; children, he thought, must learn to 'unite the spiritual and the physical' and the best way to do that was through working with their hands.

The new curriculum was designed so that it could be adjusted with the child's changing nature as each individual matured, responding to the rhythms of their development, in an early version of what we now call child-centred learning.

Academic and practical classes were valued equally in Steiner's educational vision – and craft is still compulsory – as the physical is felt to balance the intellectual in the development of every child.

Much of the writings attributed to Rudolf Steiner are from his talks and lectures in the 1920s, of which, in his *Handwork and Handicrafts – Indications by Rudolf Steiner*, he proposed rules on the learning of colours and art to promote development of a child's aesthetic sense. 'Children who learn while they are young to make practical things by hand in an artistic way, and for the benefit of others as well as for themselves, will not be strangers to life or to other people when they are older. They will be able to form their lives and their relationships in social and artistic ways, so that their lives are thereby enriched. Out of their ranks can come technicians and artists who will know how to solve the problems and tasks set us by life... But simple needlework, on the other hand, in imitation of what grown up people do, prepares both hand and heart for later life.'

Steiner also understood the transferable skills of craft and their impact on the brain, '...it is not the head alone but the whole human being that is a logician, you will, I think, be ready to appreciate in a new way the significance of lessons that demand manual or bodily skill. For it is no mere whim that has led us to require boys as well as girls to learn knitting, and so forth. Activities of this kind performed by the hand lead to an enhancement of the faculty of judgment.'

Steiner thought beauty and usefulness should be combined in objects, and that the development of a child's aesthetic sense would benefit them in adulthood. From the age of twelve, knitting was introduced to the classroom for all children, in the belief that, 'There are many people in the world who have no idea how much healthy logic and clear thinking can be developed through learning to knit. All the boys in the Waldorf schools knit a face-flannel and darn their own socks, just as the girls do. Whoever wants to be a good philosopher ought to know how to mend his shoes too.'

Unlike sloyd, where woodwork became the preferred medium, Steiner schools embrace all kinds of crafts using natural materials. Steiner divided crafts into those using soft and hard materials and attributed different benefits to each, though knitting aside – these tended to go along gender divides, amongst the teachers as well as students.

Steiner schools advocate that handiwork and practical arts are part of their curriculum, not just to develop aesthetic confidence and dexterity, but also the will, following the theory that 'The will is the power within us that allows us, though our deeds, to interact with the world. But most importantly, this *will* activity lays the foundation for our thinking.'[9]

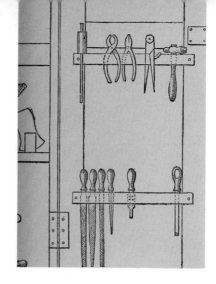

Tool cupbard from *The Teacher's Hand-book of Slöjd*, Otto Salomon, 1900.

There are many Steiner schools still in operation, with over 1,000 in 64 countries, including Japan and the US – although some in the UK have had difficulty fitting in with the current system of educational standards so have had to close in recent years.

Camphill Communities

These are homes for adults with learning difficulties, where each member has a valuable role to play as part of the whole. In a Camphill Community, residents live in 'family' house groups with a 'house parent', who is now a professional care manager. The first Camphill Community was established at Kirkton House, near Aberdeen, in 1939 by Dr Karl König, who had fled Austria in 1939, along with a group of other people who were interested in anthroposophy. The mentally handicapped, as they were called back then, wouldn't have been expected to receive any kind of education at that time, but would have been housed in hospitals and institutions, or stayed quietly – or not so quietly – at home.

Camphill is based on the philosophy of Rudolf Steiner, so craft and environment have a significant role to play in everyday life. Making bread in the dedicated bakery for the whole community is a group activity, as is growing herbs, fruit and vegetables, and performing household chores. The Camphill educational principles are based on taking into account the individual so that each person can realise their full potential.

This is achieved through holistic, whole-person curative education, which includes various therapeutic activities, including craft. There is usually a weaver in each establishment, where creative fibre crafts are encouraged as part of the regular weekly programme and where all the contributions are valued and everyone enjoys a sense of purpose. The passing of the seasons and the many Christian festivals, such as Advent, Imbolc and Candlemas, all help to mark a regular calendar and routine, something that is often so crucial to the neurodiverse, who may be resistant to change.

König said in a talk in 1943 that in Camphill there is 'no special method, but the attitude towards the children is entirely different... And this attitude matters. The schools are not called "for backward or defective children" but for children who need special care. And this is one main point. We do not consider these children backward, but different from the so-called normal ones.'[10] Camphill continues to support each person, viewing them as individuals who possess a different kind of intelligence.

Spatial awareness and difference

There is a stereotype of the disorganised professor, invariably a man, who trips over his shoes and loses his glasses. Just as we are familiar with this academic who may have little bodily intelligence, or even dyspraxia, it is also possible the other way around: that an individual with little academic achievement or a low IQ can have other skills.

Howard Gardner, he of the multiple intelligences theory, in his book *The Frames of Mind*,[11] talks about those with some cognitive deficits in one area having more competencies in another, and that a learning disability may not preclude artist talent or spatial intelligence. It is his belief that 'With these idiots savants and victims of autism, we encounter once again the flowering of a single intelligence in the face of an otherwise meagre array of abilities.' That idea was published in 1983, and we know a lot more about autistic spectrum disorders now – and how we talk about them – which may include atypical cognitive and sensory processing. This can include hypersensitivity to touch, sound and other stimuli, but also hyposensitivity, or a lack of response.

It was the Warnock Report in 1978 that suggested that children with special educational needs (SEN) may have different needs in different ways over time that are not reflected in a one-off IQ test of intelligence. Education, Health and Care Plans (EHCPs), designed to support such children in schools, replaced the older Statement of Special Educational Needs in 2014, though they are still notoriously hard to access. According to the Department of Education, the number of EHCPs in England in January 2022 was 473,255, up from 430,697 (+9.9 per cent) in 2021, and it is steadily increasing. That's 4 per cent of children in England. The percentage of pupils with SEN but no EHC plan (that is with no SEN support) has increased to 12.6 per cent.

So, there are a lot of people who are neurodivergent or have special needs in other ways, who can be supported through hands-on experiences rather than rote learning. In his book *The Arts and the Creation of Mind*,[12] Elliot Eisner wrote: 'The arts have an important role to play in refining our sensory system and cultivating our imaginative abilities. Indeed, the arts provide a kind of permission to pursue qualitative experience in a particularly focussed way and to engage in the constructive exploration of what the imaginative process may engender.'

Forest School Prospectus Whitwell Hall in Reepham, Norfolk

Outdoor education

The outdoor education movement is based on the idea of experiential learning, which is not directed and teacher-led in a classroom but involves 'learning by doing'. Ideas of woodcraft and the moral superiority of the outdoor life were inspired by a romantic notion of the life of Native Americans.

Ernest Thompson Seton (1860–1946) founded the Woodcraft Indians in 1902, which was a precursor of the Boy Scouts of America. His handbook, *The Book of Woodcraft and Indian Lore*, was published in 1912, in which he declared, 'Consumption, the white man's plague since he has become a house race, is vanquished by the sun and air and many ills of the mind also are forgotten when the sufferer boldly takes to the life in tents.'

Seton founded the Woodcraft League of America that went on to have a wide influence through his writing. On a book tour Seton gave a copy of his book, *The Birch-Bark Roll*,[13] to Lord Robert Baden-Powell, who went on to found the Boy Scouts movement in the UK.

Forest Schools

Also inspired by the ideas of Seton, Ernest Westlake founded the Order of Woodcraft Chivalry in 1916. His idea for the original Forest School was eventually realised by his son, Aubrey Westlake, opening at Sandy Balls in the New Forest, in 1929. An early prospectus for the school states its aims:

At the Forest School the Child is brought into touch with realities and is helped by a practical pursuit of the primitive arts to realise that he can learn by doing. The teaching of subjects required for exams is not neglected, but is made subsidiary to the development of a healthy grasp of real life.[14]

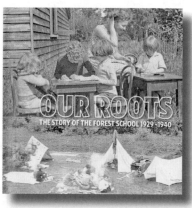

The Forest School moved to Whitwell Hall in Reepham, Norfolk, in 1938 and eventually closed down in 1940, after the outbreak of the Second World War, with children and staff evacuated to Dartington School in Devon. However, they continued to run summer camps that later became Forest School Camps and which still use the phrase Blue Sky as a greeting. This phrase had originated in Seton's writing: 'Our watchword is "Blue Sky". For under the blue sky in the sunlight, we seek to live our lives; and our thoughts are of "blue sky", for that means "cheer"; and when there are clouds, we know that the blue sky is ever behind them, and will come again.'

The Forest School[15] groups we see in schools in the UK today originated in Denmark, but became popular in the UK in the 1970s and '80s, as a reaction to the introduction of the National Curriculum in 1989 in the UK, with its attendant testing regime and key stages that are followed by the Office for Standards in Education (Ofsted). A teacher training programme for Forest Schools is well-established in the UK, allowing for more programmes to be set up within schools, and so more young people are benefitting from experiential learning.

Today in the UK we also have the Council for Learning Outside the Classroom,[16] a charity promoting 'learning experiences outdoors and away from home to enhance academic attainment and personal development', though the battle for teachers to acheive the funding, resources and relevant permissions to make trips a reality goes on.

Lord Robert Baden-Powell founded the Scout movement in the UK, which had its first camp experiment on Brownsea Island, in Dorset, in 1907. Baden-Powell is controversial for his militaristic right-wing views, though the Scouts is now a successful international movement. Their website promises that it is 'Empowering young people with skills to create a better world'. There's that idea of skills and citizenship again, which may sound familiar by now. Many other progressive educational groups appeared at this time too, such as Grith Fyrd (or Peace Army), Summerhill, Kibbo Kift and the Woodcraft Folk, among others.

Ruskin Mill

Founded in 1981, the Ruskin Mill Trust (RMT) has a curriculum based on Practical Skills Therapeutic Education (PSTE). Young people with mild to moderate learning difficulties, behavioural problems or who struggle with the classroom environment benefit from a holistic education that encourages flexible thinking. Building on the ideas of Steiner about developing the will, transformation is learned as the learner transforms materials.

The Ruskin Mill Trust now has twelve sites across the UK, and each one has its own signature craft associated with the location – from textiles in Gloucestershire, glass in Stourbridge and silversmithing and forging in Sheffield.[17]

Reflection is built in as part of the learning, and this reflective process has therapeutic benefits: 'The concept is to create a capacity for a human to reflect on him/herself without blame and therefore effectively change and dissolve unproductive and negative habits, beliefs and opinions. This in turn leads to the ability to control one's bodily impulses and urges which may be creating stress and problems within one's life.'[18]

In 2008 the RMT commissioned Aric Sigman to review their practical curriculum, and his paper, 'Practically Minded: The Benefits and Mechanisms Associated with a Craft-based Curriculum',[19] lauded the transferable value of this form of education and linked it to positive employment outcomes. Sigman also reviewed some of the new research into neurology, associating physical manipulation of objects with improved cognitive development, not just for young people with learning difficulties, but for all students. Sigman advocates life-long learning, as making also helps to stave off mental decline in later years; so carrying on with your hobby is good for your brain too.

Venture Arts ᵔᵔ

story
Venture Arts

 This award-winning visual arts charity based in Hulme, Manchester, was established in 1997 with a mission to shape a new cultural landscape where people with learning disabilities can reach their full potential as artists, curators, critics, audiences and participants. It advocates a vision of a world where learning disabled people are empowered, celebrated, included and valued in arts, culture and society.

The charity works with people of all ages. For children, there is the Schools Project, which runs ten-week art projects in both mainstream and Special Educational Needs and Disability (SEND) schools across the city. Sessions are led by Venture Arts professional artists and co-facilitated by fully trained artistic mentors who have a learning disability. That is important for several reasons; for the children, being taught by learning disabled mentors helps to break down stereotypes, change attitudes and show what is possible, while for the mentors themselves, it is meaningful, rewarding, paid work.

'In Manchester, only four per cent of learning disabled people do any sort of work,' says Venture Arts' Director, Amanda Sutton. 'But work is a basic human right, it is good for us. It makes us feel validated.'

Horace Lindezey, David Frost Ceramics 2021

Image courtesy of Venture Arts

The Young People's Art Club, based at Venture Arts' own space, is open to learning disabled young people aged eight to 25. The young adults who attend are generally those whose artistic talent can't be served elsewhere. Many of them carry on into the adult programme, which is an art studio with a serious intent. 'Local social services do sometimes send us people who have no interest in art because they see us a safe space,' Amanda says. 'And we are, of course, but

47

it only works for people who have a real need to make art. Art making is only good for you if you're interested.'

Those who are interested are supported by Venture Arts' team of professional artist tutors to discover and develop their unique artistic identity using a range of art mediums from illustration, photography and moving image to textiles, printing and ceramics. There is professional development support, too, with artists being helped to grow their portfolios and CVs, identify residences, gain commissions, sell their work and secure other paid creative work.

'The people who are here tend to stay a long time,' says Amanda. 'It takes a lot of encouragement, support and care to help them explore their creativity. We also work hard to make sure both they and their artwork gets out into the wider world through initiatives such as our Cultural Enrichment programme, [a guided work experience programme where participants work alongside teams in cultural institutions to gain a greater understanding of the day-to-day running of a museum or gallery], exhibitions and events. The barriers to learning disabled people in life in general are still huge, but through the work we do, we are seeing our artists being recognised and appreciated by the art world.'

Portrait of Horace Lindezey photo Becky Hislop

Horace

Horace Lindezey is one of those artists. This is his story:

Horace Lindezey is a skilled illustrator, textile artist, photographer and ceramicist, whose work depicts the world around him, his family and his memories of growing up in inner-city Manchester. He has been at Venture Arts since the beginning, having left school at a time when arts and crafts were seen as a way to keep learning disabled people busy. In the more than three decades since, Horace's work has been exhibited in leading art institutions across the UK, including Pallant House in Chichester, The Lowry in Manchester, and Sotheby's in London.

Horace Lindezey,
The Seven Suits, wire
drawings on sheet
metal, 2016
image courtesy of Venture Arts

The son of a carpenter father and seamstress mother, Horace was
familiar with making from a young age. He remembers his mother
sewing bridesmaids' dresses in their living room and watching as
she hand-stitched tiny beads to the fabric. He wasn't allowed to
touch anything at the time, but later, when he was introduced
to a sewing machine at Venture Arts, he knew exactly what to do.
His sewing skills have developed further at Venture Arts and he
is now an accomplished stitcher, both on the machine and by hand.
'The way Horace works is really intricate,' says Amanda Sutton.
'It's important to him to sit and do things quietly.'

Horace is fascinated by weddings and wedding dresses (as well
as other 'special occasional days', as he calls them, such as
christenings and funerals). He has created beautiful embroidered
pictures of the weddings of some of his favourite television
characters, including Scott and Charlene from *Neighbours* and Roy
and Hayley Cropper from *Coronation Street*, and he has made
a series of miniature wedding dress sculptures from fabric which
he then dips in porcelain. The process of making these delicate
pieces has become a ceremony in itself, as Horace recites words
remembered from weddings he has seen.

49

Clay is a material Horace returns to again and again. 'The clay feels soft and I just let my hands and the clay decide the shape,' he says. He has recently been working on a series of free-form coil pots decorated with drawings of churches, one of which was shown as part of the 2022 'Brick by Brick: Architectures of Potential' exhibition at Manchester's Portico Library, but he is perhaps best known for his clay plaques. These reworkings of the familiar Blue Plaques that adorn the facades of many of London's buildings in honour of the notable men and women who once lived or worked in them, commemorate both people Horace has known personally, including his father, Wilston Lindezey, and Shine the Taxi Driver, in addition to well-known characters from the 1980s. 'One, shown at the Whitworth Art Gallery as part of the Manchester Element of the British Art Show 2021, reads: *David Frost, 1939–2013. He was on breakfast TV while I ate my cornflakes and drank me cup of tea.* Another, which was shown in 2023 as part of the national touring exhibition 'Humanity', curated by arts charity Outside In, is dedicated to *Grange Hill* star Danny Kendall.

'Horace has so much interest and creativity,' says Amanda Sutton. Venture Arts has enabled him to develop that into a serious art practice. 'I come to Venture Arts to learn and study,' Horace explains. 'I don't want to stay in the house all the time. I feel good here. Doing speeches with Amanda and having my art in galleries makes me feel proud. I am an artist.'

Above: Lasmin Salmon, Cushion Quilt, Thread, Elysium Gallery, 2021

photo: Hew Maddock

story
ActionSpace

ActionSpace is an exceptional visual arts development agency for learning disabled artists. Based in three separate studios across London, the agency aims to make a professional career in the visual arts a realistic option for learning disabled artists by unlocking talent, creating opportunities and realising potential.

'We work with people who are serious about being artists,' explains ActionSpace's Co-Director, Sheryll Catto. 'And we work specifically with adults because when people with learning disabilities leave school they are, in general, unable to access art school curriculums. That means they need an alternative way of developing their practices in a studio environment, and support to access professional opportunities.'

ActionSpace takes art-making seriously. Their artists attend weekly studio sessions where they work alongside specialist artist facilitators whose role is to support them to develop their individual practice and establish their own unique artistic signatures.

These sessions take place in dedicated spaces based in three professional art studios: Studio Voltaire in Clapham, Cockpit, Bloomsbury and ASC Ealing Road in Brent, which are used by internationally acclaimed artists including 2016 Turner Prize shortlisted Anthea Hamilton. 'Being part of a professional studio is really important,' Sheryll says. 'It means that our artists are a part of the contemporary art world and are working alongside other artists who understand them.'

Some ActionSpace artists come simply to make work, but for those who wish to, there are also many opportunities to exhibit and to sell. The Exhibition Programme provides every artist with at least one opportunity to exhibit each year and there is also a professional Artist Development programme, run in partnership with a range of contemporary arts organisations, which aims to provide artists with the same opportunities and experiences as their non-learning disabled peers.

'A lot of what we do at ActionSpace is think about how to make things possible,' Sheryll explains. 'We are here to do the bridging, to make it easy for our artists to make art and function as professional artists, and also to help galleries and other visual arts organisations become more diverse and inclusive. Many of our artists spend their lives looking through the eyes of people who are just looking at their limitations – they have to go to numerous evaluation meetings where most of the talk is about what they can't do. So to succeed – to have work exhibited and bought – can change their sense of self and open up their lives. There is always a wonderful moment at an exhibition when the family comes in and sees a piece of artwork and they suddenly see the person's abilities and understand that they are an artist. That's really important.'

Lasmin

Textile artist Lasmin Salmon has been working at ActionSpace for more than two decades and her joyously coloured, mixed media, sewn sculptures have been exhibited in a number of group shows, including 'Thread' at Swansea's Elysium Gallery, in 2021, where she showed alongside textile artists Shelly Goldsmith, Raisa Kabir and Shona Robin, and the national touring exhibition 'Radical Craft', in 2016. Lasmin was also commissioned to develop an installation titled 'Yarn Mountain' with fellow textile artist Celia

Lasmin Salmon in the ActionSpace studio at Studio Voltaire, 2019

image courtesy of the Artist and ActionSpace
photo: Charlotte Hollinshead

Pym for the 2014 'Festival of Love' at the Southbank Centre in London. This is her story:

Lasmin has limited verbal skills and works with artist facilitator Charlotte Hollinshead at Studio Voltaire, where ActionSpace's south London studio is based. 'We haven't taught her anything in terms of practical skills,' Charlotte says, 'her mum was a seamstress, and she could already knit when she first came here. What we have done as facilitators is enable her to shape what she was already doing into a serious art practice, so, rather than being manoeuvred into different craft projects – knitting a scarf, making a quilt, etc. – she now initiates her own projects.'

Those projects are months, and sometimes years, in the making, and Lasmin often explores several ideas at once, playing with materials, bending and twisting fabrics, before settling on a style and shape that she feels connected with. She then recreates that shape in many varied forms, meticulously constructing each piece

Lasmin Salmon, Rug (detail), 2014

image courtesy of the Artist and ActionSpace

with carefully selected fabrics, pulling them through her fingers to ensure they are the right texture, pattern or weight before embarking on a new piece.

While she is predominantly led by her physical relationship with her material, Lasmin is also constantly exploring ways to exhibit her work. Several years ago, she created a series of small, circular, sewn sculptures, which she nailed to the wall, creating a different arrangement every time. (When they were shown as part of the 2013 'Side by Side' exhibition directed by artist Alice Fox, Lasmin chose to set them out around a pillar where they resembled a cluster of exotic sea anemones.) For the 2021 Thread exhibition, her giant quilt made from multiple individual cushion forms was stretched out as a three-dimensional painting across one of the gallery walls.

During the Covid-19 pandemic lockdowns of 2020 and 2021, Lasmin spent a lot of time knitting at home. When she returned to the studio, she brought the knitted lengths with her and since then has been carefully repairing them, stitching into them and patching them with circles of fabric. 'We don't know yet what she is going to do with them,' Charlotte says, 'but like all her work, the colours are amazing, and she likes hanging them over clothes rails and putting them on herself and other people.'

This interactive element of Lasmin's work is important. Charlotte is keen to make clear that Lasmin has a professional art practice and that her art-making is not a form of therapy. However, she does acknowledge that for Lasmin, more than many artists, her work is an opportunity for her to expand her communication.

'Lasmin's work has the capacity to provide her with the space to explore her communication creatively.' Charlotte says. 'She needs to work independently and be in control of her practice but she also wants to share her work and she loves the break-out moments when something she has made enables a playful exchange with other people.'

story
Intoart

 Established in 2000 and led by co-founders Ella Ritchie MBE and Sam Jones, Intoart is a pioneering visual arts organisation that champions its founding vision for people with learning disabilities to be visible, equal and established artists and designers.

Located in the heart of Peckham, Intoart's studio has been embedded within the communities of south London for the past 23 years. The full-time studio programme spans art, design and craft and is an alternative art school where people with learning disabilities are able to develop a long-term creative practice.

'We aim to shift the perception of art and design made by people with learning disabilities from solely "therapeutic activity" towards investing in meaningful, useful production, whose outcomes are equitable in ambition, conceptual relevance and aesthetic pleasure to any artists, maker or designers' practice,' explains Ella Ritchie. 'Assumptions prevail that people with learning disabilities are the recipients of a service and are participants rather than contemporary cultural producers in their own right. There is a huge amount of work still to be done to raise expectations and challenge preconceptions. We believe that with increased ambition, the artwork made by artists from Intoart is a strong counter to those prejudices.'

Putting the work that their artists make out into the world is a vital part of that ambition. They have their own 'Intoart Collection', a publicly accessible loaning resource for curators, researchers, writers and organisations that contains more than 5,000 original artworks made in the Intoart studio, and have realised exhibitions and commissions with contemporary art galleries and museums across the world. They also work with their artists towards successful acquisitions by the Arts Council Collection, the Victoria and Albert Museum, Crafts Council Collection and the Government Art Collection, and have supported them to enter – and win – several prestigious awards.

Christian Ovonlen

photo Alun Callender

Christian

One of those award-winning artists is Christian Ovonlen. This is his story:

Christian Ovonlen joined Intoart in 2013, where he developed a practice inspired by his interest in pop visual culture and the history of fashion and costume. His work has been exhibited in a number of group exhibitions, including 'Fashioning Space' at the Victoria and Albert Museum as part of London Design Festival 2017, and in 2022 he presented his 'Ballets Russes' series of theatrical hand-painted, hand-dyed silks at Collect, the International Fair for Contemporary Craft and Design.

These large-scale hanging panels, with their intricate, fluid and vividly coloured gestural marks, were met with widespread acclaim; the Victoria and Albert Museum acquired them for their permanent collection and Christian was named winner of the Brookfield Properties Craft Award 2022. Created in partnership with the Crafts Council, this annual prize commends the achievements of a maker who has significantly shaped the story and success of craft across the UK. 'We were immediately blown away by the colours and

Feathered Cape (II) 2023, Christian Ovonlen photo: Alun Callender

movement in Christian's work,' said the curatorial director of
Brookfield Properties, Saff Williams. 'His figures appear to lift off
the silks, dancing across the fabric, bold in line and brushwork.'

Christian's creative process begins in research. Inspired by sources
found in archives, museum collections, popular culture and nature,
he sketches on paper before translating his designs onto silk textiles
using handcrafted print techniques. 'I do drawings, blending the
colours on the papers, turquoise blues and bright blues, the browns
and the greens,' he explains. 'I always like pink, orangey yellow
and pinky yellow. I like doing black, shiny ink on tracing paper to
make a pattern and then choosing the ink colours. On the screens,
I use the paint brushes, thin, thick and medium. I enjoy doing the
squeegee. When I take the screen off, I see it's going to be amazing
and wonderful.'

Christian's practice is constantly developing. The final piece in
the 'Ballets Russes' series, 'Girl with Feathered Cape', led him to
experiment with making textiles and costumes that he can wear.
He drew the shape with its curved collar, flowing cape and full-
length underdress on paper by hand, then reproduced it on a
pattern-cutter's dress pattern. This enabled him to work directly
with the lengths of silk, using the painting techniques he developed
so successfully for the panels. 'When I'm wearing my work it looks
like I am wearing a uniform,' he says. 'In the future, I want to
be making more costumes and outfits. If I make lots of costumes,
it looks like I am doing a catwalk.'

Intoart's director Ella Ritchie believes the award is a well-deserved 'testament to Christian's contribution to craft alongside other internationally recognised makers'.

Christian himself says he is 'happy and excited to win awards', but his sense of fulfilment lies in the work itself. 'Work makes me happy,' he says. 'Amazing, wonderful, marvellous, gorgeous, beautiful colours. I look closely at my drawings, drawing the stage with browns, the dancers with black shoes. I close my eyes and imagine being at the theatre, in the audience scared of the dark and then happy when the stage lights shine. The dancers are dancing on the stage, I am hearing classical music. The dancers in my silks are like a melody.'

Learning on the job

Apprenticeships were the traditional way for a young person to learn a trade, at the service of a master of their trade. For this experience, parents would pay a craft or tradesman an indenture, often from a young age. Standards were governed by the local guilds, and after several years an apprentice could qualify as a Journeyman, from the French journée, meaning they could now charge for a day's work. Eventually they would make a 'masterpiece' that would be submitted to see if they could reach the standard of Master Craftsman.

Modern apprentices are overseen by the Institute for Apprenticeships and Technical Education, who describe their occupational standards as the 'knowledge, skills and behaviours' (KSBs) needed to be competent in a job. Formed in association with employers, these apprenticeships comprise 80 per cent hands-on training and 20 per cent teaching from a local college or provider. This works well for larger businesses, but one of the problems in the creative sector is that craftspeople often work alone, so committing to educate a young person, including taking the time to teach them, is often not practically possible. The Queen Elizabeth Scholarship Trust (QEST) offers funding to help micro-businesses and sole traders afford the salary to be able to pay a trainee in crafts. In 2022, Heritage Crafts launched some pre-apprenticeship taster courses, funded and run with Penwith Landscape Partnership, to give young people aged 16 to 25 the opportunity to have a go at Cornish hedging, basketry or coppersmithing.

story
Apprenticeships

 'Person-to-person teaching is vital to saving endangered crafts because there are so many skills that simply can't be articulated through language or recording. And the best form of person-to-person teaching is the apprentice model – one master craftsperson with one trainee, hands-on in the workplace.'

Those are the words of Daniel Carpenter, Executive Director of Heritage Crafts, the advocacy body for traditional heritage crafts. In recent years, Daniel has seen first-hand the impact of the decline in craft education in schools and the shift from practical to theoretical learning models in higher education. His members report that young people are leaving school with no idea that craft-based careers are even possible, and that graduates of craft-based degree courses are entering the workplace with so few hand skills that their employers must train them from scratch.

Heritage Crafts is doing all it can to change this and to help re-introduce a broader sense of education. They were on the advisory board for the Craft and Design T level, which is due to be launched in September 2024 with the aim of creating parity with academic learning (a T level is the equivalent of three A levels) and are also helping to set up a National Craft Skills Academy. This residential centre would enable apprentices to do all the required classroom training in a single six-to-eight-week block rather than on day release at a Further Education college or specialist centre. 'The Institute of Apprenticeships has indicated that there are precedents for this kind of front-loaded training in other sectors, so the Academy could become a reality within the next couple of years.'

And in spring 2023 they launched their second pre-apprenticeship programme in Countryside Crafts. At the time of writing, this Cornwall-based project was in its infancy, but it followed a very successful pilot that Heritage Crafts ran in west Somerset in 2017, funded by a grant from the Ernest Cook Trust. That programme saw three crafts practitioners – papermaker Jim Patterson,

Papermaking at Two Rivers Paper, Somerset. Cotton rag is pre-beaten for strength, as demonstrated by Zoe

basketmaker Sarah Webb and green woodworker Stefan Jennings – each take on three young people in their workshops for a period of six weeks. The craftspeople were paid fairly for their time and the students got a taste of what a career in heritage crafts could be like, as well as a transferable basic-level NVQ qualification in employability skills. 'The idea was to take the risk out for both sides,' Daniel explains. 'For the crafts person, it removed the financial risk of spending six weeks with a young person and it not working out, and for the young person, it alleviated the psychological and emotional risk of stepping over the threshold into somewhere very alien.'

Zoe

One of those young people was Zoe Collis, who, after completing the pre-apprenticeship programme with Stefan Jennings, was taken on by Jim Patterson as a full-time papermaking apprentice. After three years of on-the-job training, combined with day release at a local college, Zoe was awarded her Level 3 qualification in February 2021 and is now a Journeyman Papermaker at Patterson's Two Rivers Papers in the coastal town of Watchet, Somerset. This is her story:

It was my absolute refusal to go to university that got me onto the pre-apprenticeship scheme. I believed then, and still do, that university is not accommodating to all minds.

I am great in the classroom, but I really struggle in exams. I was an arty child, but my parents were adamant that I focused on maths and science because they believed I was more likely to secure a good job with STEM qualifications. I respected that, so I took engineering rather than art at GCSE and when I went to college to do my A levels, I chose psychology, sociology, geography and chemistry. But I soon realised that I just couldn't cope with the exams, so I dropped chemistry and picked up graphic design in my second year. Things snowballed from there. I found myself focusing more and more on design and sculpting, so I decided to stay on and do a Foundation Diploma in Arts, Media and Design.

My parents and tutors were still hoping I might go to university, but I was really, really stubborn. I was using quite physical materials for my projects rather than just paint, and for one assessment I made a series of objects out of Plasticine. The work was dexterous and sculptural and that was when everyone began to take my choice to work with my hands seriously.

The Heritage Crafts' pre-apprenticeship scheme had just launched and I was lucky enough to be chosen to take part. I was sent off to work with the green woodworker Stefan Jennings. I made furniture with him, I wove willow with him – it was only one a day a week but I was captivated. Working with willow was what I wanted to do.

Unfortunately, when the work experience came to an end, Stefan couldn't take me on as an apprentice. I met up with the pre-apprenticeship scheme's Project Manager, Tracy Hill, who was determined to find me a job. Opportunities near where I live in rural Somerset were limited and the only craft job available was at Two Rivers Paper.

I didn't know anything about papermaking and I was plunged straight into the deep end, so it was a sharp learning curve. Two Rivers Paper specialise in handmade rag paper – that's paper made from cotton and linen rather than wood pulp – for artists and

**Zoe Collis,
Papermaking at Two
Rivers Paper,** Somerset.
'We have seen the
future… and it's called
Zoe,' Jim Patterson

designers. It's one of only a handful of commercial hand-mills
operating in Europe and the company has been run by Jim since
1988. He's been making paper all his life.

I don't believe in fate, but it does feel like this job was meant
for me. Papermaking is part craft, part art and part science, and
I'm involved in every stage of the process. I find looking at the
finished sheets of paper, knowing that I have made them and that
they will go off to all corners of the world, extremely rewarding.

Artists sometimes send me paintings as a thank you and knowing that I have been part of that person's art feels incredible. No other job opportunities I've ever seen offer that.

An apprenticeship is the only way to learn a craft like papermaking. It requires dexterity and you can't understand the process unless you've had your elbows steeped in the cotton. The techniques required to make paper are very esoteric and there are thousands of years of technology in its evolution. It's so common that people take it for granted, but where would we be without paper? I am a Journeyman now, which means I am qualified and experienced but not yet outstanding enough to be a master papermaker. That is a bit humbling, but I hope to be more than Journeyman one day.

T levels

The new T levels are the practical version of A levels, a two-year option for post-16 students designed to support their progression and meet the needs of employers. Within these, every student has an industry placement to gain experience. Around 10,200 new students were introduced to T levels in 2022, studying subjects such as Business and Administration, Construction, Digital, Engineering and Manufacturing, Finance, Education and Healthcare Science.

The efficacy of T levels has yet to be seen, though it's good that something is on the table. Due to be launched in 2024 are T levels in Hairdressing, Barbering and Beauty Therapy; Craft and Design; and Media, Broadcast and Production. These pathways have been postponed by a year to enable further industry consultation. The awarding organisation, the Northern Council for Further Education (NCFE), say the specialisms available will be jewellery, textiles and fashion, ceramics and furniture making. The creative skills that are developed in the Craft and Design pathway include:

- Lateral thinking
- Making novel connections
- Handling ambiguity
- Taking acceptable risks
- Forming ideas iteratively
- Future proofing

The value of creativity

Craft makes a massive economic contribution to the value of the creative industries. Everyone wants things that are crafted and authentic. The luxury market for handmade, high-end purchases is experiencing a growth, while both amateur crafting and the romantic ideal of rural 'crafting from home' entrepreneurship are in overdrive. In 2019, the Creative Industries contributed £116 billion in Gross Value Added (i.e., the value of goods and services produced), growing twice as fast between 2011 and 2019 than the rate of the UK economy as a whole.[20] It also accounted for 2.3 million jobs.

Despite all this, GCSE uptake for creative subjects is low, and getting lower. A BBC survey in January 2018[21] showed that nine out of ten secondary schools had cut back on lesson time, staff or facilities in at least one

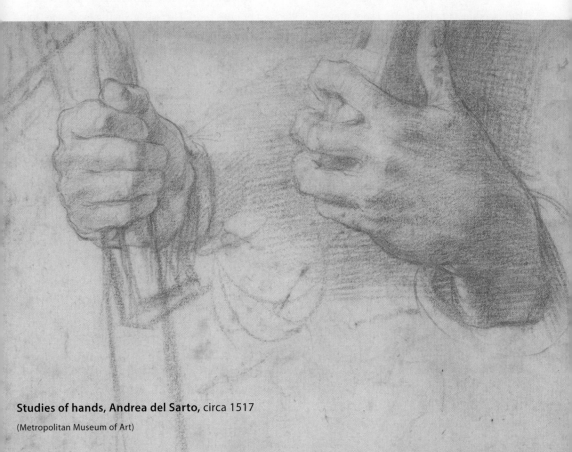

Studies of hands, Andrea del Sarto, circa 1517
(Metropolitan Museum of Art)

creative arts subject. The English Baccalaureate (EBacc) system, which encourages the grouping of subjects that the government says are 'important', excludes the arts.

If young people don't study these subjects at GCSE, they won't study them at A level. Since 2014, the number of A level entries in arts subjects – which include drama, music and art – in England has fallen by 13,000; that's almost 17 per cent.

Higher education is affected too; many graduate craft courses have closed, while others have been amalgamated into 'Contemporary Crafts' degrees, meaning it's hard to study ceramics at this level in the UK. The Crafts Council[22] says craft courses in Higher Education dropped by 54 per cent between 2007/08 and 2015/16.

The promised Cultural Education plan, announced by the Department for Culture, Media and Sport (DCMS)[23] in 2022, has been subject to several delays, so we have yet to see any plan.

The Arts Council Strategy in April 2020[24] aims to create a nation of creators so children can fulfil their creative potential. The Arts Council invests in portfolio providers, as well as a raft of bridge organisations that are creating local education partnerships across the country. 'We will make the case for a stronger focus on teaching for creativity and critical thinking across the curriculum, both to school leaders and to the Department for Education. Employers from all industries and sectors spoke [in research] of the value they placed on creative skills and critical thinking in their workforces, and over the next decade we will work to ensure that those skills are developed more effectively in young people. In addition, we are committed to ensuring that a broad and vital arts curriculum is taught in all schools.'

The Arts Council acknowledges the softer benefits too: 'There is growing evidence that creative and cultural activity can lead to improved health and wellbeing.' In their 2022 Creative Health and Wellbeing manifesto, they promise to 'promote creative health as a fundamental part of living well'. Part of this has been the creation of the Culture, Health and Wellbeing Alliance: a sector support organisation to share research and good practice.

A skills index report from City & Guilds found a mismatch between the skills provided by schools and the needs of business. Just over half of businesses reported being able to recruit people with the skills they needed, which include those human, soft skills such as interpersonal and problem solving.

There is evidence that craft skills benefit people in other ways, too. Professor Dame Julia King, Baroness Brown of Cambridge, is an engineer who specialises in

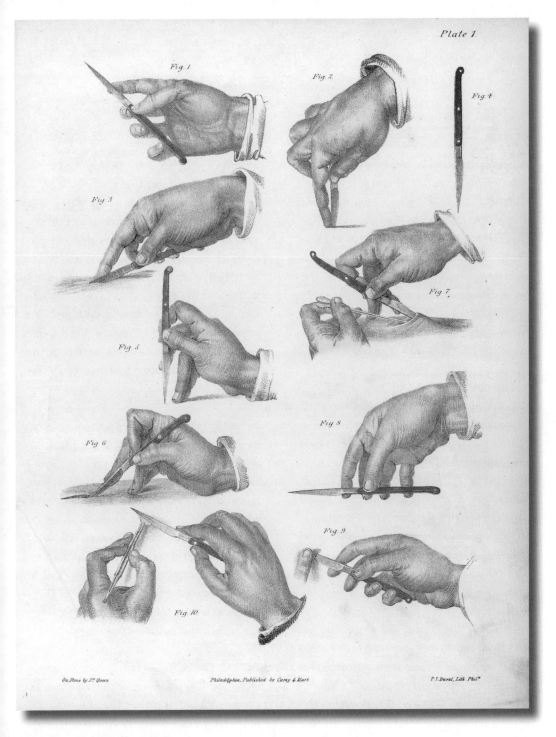

Illustration of operative surgery

Joseph Pancoast, 1846 photo: Wellcome Trust

manipulating metals. Interviewed on *The Life Scientific*, on BBC Radio 4, Professor King told theoretical physicist and presenter Jim Al-Khalili how the dressmaking skills she learnt from her mother as a child helped her to understand the composite structures used in wind turbines later in life. She believes it was the visual-spatial skills acquired from turning a two-dimensional paper pattern into a three-dimensional structure that enabled her to make that leap.

In his book *Expert*, the surgeon Roger Kneebone has noted the lack of basic skills in medical students. 'Young people entering science and medicine at our university have excellent academic results, but many struggle to tie a firm knot, cut out a shape with scissors, or speak in front of other people. Though a glance at the UK state secondary school curriculum gives a clue as to why this is, my students come from all over the world, which makes me think the problem is global.'[25]

Flexibility, imagination and originality are all valued behaviours and are more necessary today than ever. Creativity in education isn't just for the art class, it crosses all subject boundaries and is as useful in maths and science classes as it is in English or drama. However, the myth persists that creatives are mavericks or divas that need to be managed. The legend of the creative genius or temperamental artist is confronted head on by Dr Daisy Fancourt and Professor Andrew

Steptoe's research at the Department of Behavioural Science, University College London.[26] Their research looks at the effects of creativity on social behaviour in children aged seven to nine years, with an emphasis on everyday creativity through play and creative activities, what they term 'little c' creativity, as opposed to the 'Big C' of a few remarkable individuals. Their evidence didn't implicate creativity in any kind of mental illness, in fact quite the opposite seems be true, with creative activities providing protection from such problems.

In his introduction to a report commissioned by the Education Endowment Foundation, Sir Kevan Collins wrote: 'In my view, schools should still find space in their day to ensure all children benefit from a stimulating arts education. We should continue to investigate links to other outcomes we value, but we shouldn't expect everything to link tightly to academic attainment. Instead, we should teach the arts for their own sake – for the intrinsic value of learning creative skills and the enjoyment they bring.'

In 2019 The Durham Commission[27] also recommended teaching for those soft skills as well as scholarship and craftsmanship, not merely exam-passing. 'As a result of our research, we assert that the integration of teaching for creativity in our education system will result in young people who have an ability to express their creativity and have the personal creative confidence that will support them in all aspects of their lives – not just in employment and economic success, but also in their relationships with others in their community and in their own identity, health and wellbeing.'

Part of the Durham Commission's report includes all the other papers and programmes that came to the same conclusion, such as the excellent Creative Partnerships, which ran from 2002 to 2009. The programme, which established relationships between schools and local creative practitioners, was seen to positively influence students' wellbeing. Research by PricewaterhouseCoopers quoted in the *Guardian* at the time found that 'young people involved with Creative Partnerships activities achieve, on average, 2.5 grades better at GCSE than their peers in similar schools'. Despite this, the UK Government persists with an academic bias, and with the state education system under stress and underfunded, creative subjects are still a rare thing in schools. It's no accident that many of our popular creatives in public life come from the private school sector, where they are exposed to drama, arts and a broader extra-curricular environment.

Bodily intelligence

Howard Gardner was the psychologist who came up with the concept of multiple intelligences, and the idea that people don't absorb knowledge in the same ways. Instead of accepting the academic measure of intelligence quotient, or IQ, through a test,

we should perhaps think of the value of other kinds of competence. In his seminal work *Frames of Mind* [29] he doesn't blame the tests. 'The problem lies less in the technology of testing than in the ways in which we customarily think about the intellect and in our ingrained views of intelligence. Only if we expand and reformulate our view of what counts as human intellect will we be able to devise more appropriate ways of assessing it and more effective ways of educating it.'

One of Gardner's intelligences is bodily kinaesthetic, in which he includes dancers, actors and artisans. Crafts and the manipulation of tools use several intelligences at once, such as spatial as well as bodily kinaesthetic. Gardner says, 'In my own view, fine motor bodily intelligence, in combination with spatial capacities, is mostly strongly entailed in the use of objects and tools.' Gardner originally came up with six types of intelligence, while several others have been added since.

Gardner goes on to say, 'bodily intelligence completes a trio of object-related intelligences: logical-mathematical intelligence, which grows out of the patterning of objects into numerical arrays: spatial intelligence, which focuses on the individual's ability to transform objects within his environment and make his way amidst a world of objects in space; and bodily intelligence, which focusing inward, is limited to the exercise of one's own day and, facing outward, entails physical actions on the objects in the world.' His hope was that by identifying an individual's intellectual profile, or learning type, at an early age, they could be offered the most helpful kind of education.

The Crafts Council's Firing Up scheme, launched in 2011, took ceramists into schools, bought kilns and trained teachers how to use them. Firing Up was supported by a three-year grant from the Esmée Fairbairn Foundation and Paul Hamlyn Foundation. Over three years it established partnerships with eleven Higher Education Institutes in England; Firing Up reached over 55 schools with creative and inspirational opportunities to work in clay. During the programme, Sarah Cawthorn, Head of Art, Wellfield School, Sunderland, noted: 'The pupils have benefited from working with clay, because they've learnt to take more ownership of their work. I was also very surprised, as a couple of the louder children went very quiet when using clay.'

The Head of Art in the Manchester Firing Up cluster said, 'A lot of our kids don't speak English as their first language and a proportion aren't literate in their first language. Being able to express their thoughts using their hands has really improved their grades. They have produced work that they wouldn't have had the opportunity to produce, had they not been working in clay and had they not been

working in 3D. Successes in art give children the confidence to do well in other areas. They're now more confident and more excited about talking about what they've done. Attendance is better for some of those pupils. They've really engaged with our subject but they're also starting to engage more with school. So it's having a big impact on them holistically.'

Since the experience of Covid and lockdowns, many people have discovered this for themselves and had the time to create at home. Writing for the Royal Academy blog, Antony Gormley was positive.[30] 'Despite the daily pressures people have faced during lockdown, for me the most wonderful thing that has come out of this period is to see so clearly that everybody makes things. In so many homes, the family kitchen has become a studio – people have been sitting at their tables drawing and painting and making stuff. There's been a realisation that actually, everyone enjoys that sensation of messing about with a box of paints or a lump of clay.

'The cultural shift that has already seen people nurturing their own creativity in lockdown is a wonderful precursor for the big shifts that need to happen. Art is a place of radical possibility, in which anything can be imagined and then made real. What would it mean if all children grew up feeling that potential to act in and on the world?'

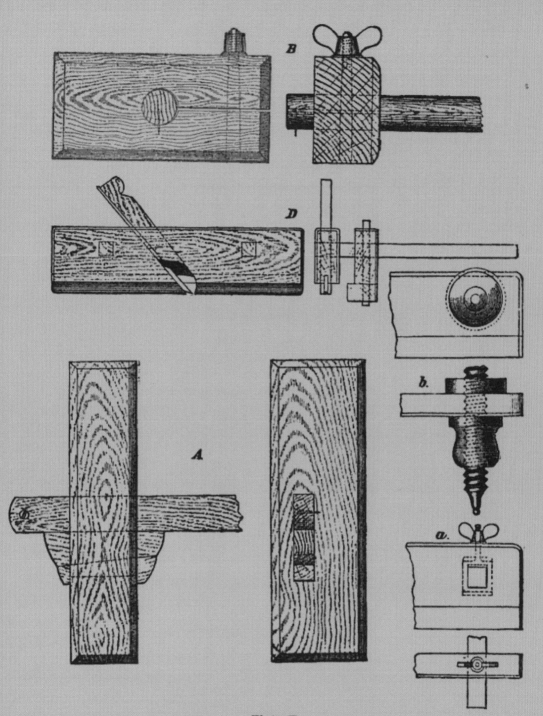

Plate X.

A. Marking gauge (Johansson's) with stock adjusted by wedges. ½.
B. Marking gauge (Lundmark's modified) with stock adjusted by thumb-screw. ½.
D. Plough-gauge, *a* and *b*, different methods of adjustment. ¼.

Woodwork gauges from *The Teacher's Hand-book of Slöjd*, Otto Salomon, 1892

story
An alternative provision

Helen Brown is an art teacher in an English alternative provision academy for children and young people aged eleven to 16 who have been excluded from mainstream school. This is her story.

'The focus here is on Science, Maths and English; art is not elevated from a structural point of view. However, post-16, young people have to either be in full-time education or on an apprenticeship and they need two GCSEs to get to college, so it is a useful GCSE for many of the children who come to us.

Essentially, the art we offer here is therapy, but we're not allowed to approach it as therapy because we have to follow a mainstream school's pathway. That means we use the model of Artist – Response – Final Outcome where we present artists, teach the techniques, understand how they put their work together, explore materials and then create something unique from it. Achieving that is hard – many of our students have never managed to sit through an art lesson from start to finish and, almost without fail, they come into my class for the first time saying they hate art and don't know why they're here. Typically, the conversation goes like this:

Me: *Right, this your art class. There are certain things we have to tick off to keep in line with the curriculum, but I'm here to ask you what you enjoy.*
Pupil: *I fuckin' hate art.*
Me: *Okay, but you have to start somewhere. So do you like drawing, painting, sculpture, clay...?*
Pupil: *I fuckin' hate clay.*
Me: *What about painting, or drawing, or tracing?*
Pupil: *I told you, I fuckin' hate art.*
Me: *What about colouring?*
Pupil: *Alright, yeah, I quite like colouring in.*

So, I'll give them a line drawing of, for example, an Air Jordan – which many of the pupils wear – and they'll colour it in. And, more often than not, they're really pleased with the result. Then I'll get

photos: Everyone's Warehouse, courtesy of Every One Every Day

them to cut it out. I'll admire it and tell them it looks a bit like this artist Michael Craig-Martin. And then we're off. The lesson model has been met, they've learned they can trust me, but the most important thing in that scenario is that they have been successful.

Success is particularly important for the children and young people who come to us. Teaching a class of six, at least two of whom are likely to have ADHD, is like spinning plates. The minute one of them 'fails', the whole stack starts to wobble. So, what we are aiming for is a settled group of students who are fully engaged in what they are doing. Art and crafts provide that engagement because they offer many ways of successful challenge; the correct level of success versus failure and the correct level of expectation that what they are doing is going to succeed. And for lots of children it has been the missing key. I can name many examples of children who have been able to move on successfully both because art was the only the GCSE they got, and also because it offered a route to engagement.

We have a crisis in our schools. Levels of challenge were rising before the Covid pandemic, but since then behaviour has fallen off a cliff across the board. Teachers are facing increasing abuse and refusal in most schools. Here, in alternative provision, the issues we are facing are unprecedented.

There are many reasons for this situation, and it is not every child by any means. However, the system I am working in is, in my opinion, not addressing the core problem – which is engagement. If, as a society, we are not going to be honest about the reasons why increasing numbers of young people are unable to accept education (and the push-back that would require), we need to fashion an alternative.

I strongly believe that the only way we can address this crisis is by encouraging participation through engagement hubs, where a child can spend most of their time progressing in a field most interesting to them, whether that is in science, language or the arts. The desire to create things is in us all, it is part of what it is to be human, we just need to show our young people what that act of positive creation can mean for them.'

Maker Movement

The next work revolution is happening right now: people can print things at home on their 3D printers and text is written by artificially intelligent bots. Are we prepared for the resilience and flexible thinking that is required to adjust to a new way of being? The Covid pandemic has hastened some of these slow evolutions, working from home is becoming the new norm and digital meetings are not a rarity.

The pandemic also meant an increasing risk of unemployment for many in an age of zero-hour contracts. It is this kind of uncertainty that we have had to adjust to, while surrounded by opaque technology that should be helping us.

Material nature

The Arts and Crafts movement of the second half of the nineteenth century was founded on simple forms, truth to material, inspiration from nature and the idea that creative manual work could improve the quality of life. These ideals were a reaction against elaborate Victorian designs and, although designer William Morris and his followers were not anti-machine per se, they did believe that industrialisation had resulted in a debasement of design and workmanship, and in reducing physical contact with materials, it had alienated people from the products of their labour. Since the Industrial Revolution the workplace had become a place of routine tasks – many performed as part of a conveyor-belt system using simple actions that could be repeated by almost anyone.

Skill was no longer required and the feedback loop of material information coming through the hands was disrupted, the worker reduced to being just a thoughtless cog in a machine. Morris' romantic views of the feudal society of indentured labourers of the past may not have been shared by those who had lived that life and, certainly, returning to some rosy-tinted idea of the past is not helpful in contemporary debate. However, based as it was on the concept of honest and functional design and the importance of creative manual work, the Arts and Crafts Movement has synergies with the contemporary Maker Movement (minus the moral baggage). An article about artisanal capitalism[31] in The Economist declared members of the new Maker Movement to be the twenty-first-century heirs of Arts and Crafts.

If industrialisation distanced people from production in the nineteenth century, new technology is now doing the opposite in the twenty-first, as 3D printing and computer-controlled machinery allow people to get back in touch with the means of production. Fab Labs – a digital fabrication laboratory – call it 'technological empowerment'.

Maker spaces are emerging all over the country, either as independent spaces or within other institutions. Many are led by groups of young people with the curiosity and energy to turn them into active, local community groups made financially sustainable through membership. A report from the RSA (Royal Society for the encouragement of Arts, Manufactures and Commerce), Ours to Master, [32] summed up their impact: 'Maker spaces have a role to play in changing our broader worldview. Put another way, they are not just sites to make craft objects but also places to champion new values and experiment witha different way of living – one that may be based on the tenets of self-reliance, sustainability and open-source thinking.'

Inclusivity has to mean allowing people to 'have a go' and learn by using their hands. These ideas were explored in Power of Making, an exhibition at the Victoria and Albert Museum, part of a three-year Crafts Council collaboration. Daniel Charny, curator of the show, wrote: 'The reality is that although most people can make, most people don't. In fact, fewer and fewer, especially those who live in cities, actually know how to make the things they use, need or want; or even how these things are made. This is one of the more dramatic and unfortunate legacies of the Industrial Revolution which has shaped the world we live in.'

The exhibition proposed the idea that making is the new thinking, and in the catalogue Martina Margetts quotes Foucault in saying philosophy today should be thinking differently. 'This exhibition shows that making is the only way that Foucault's exhortation to "think differently" can ever be tangibly experienced in everyday life.'

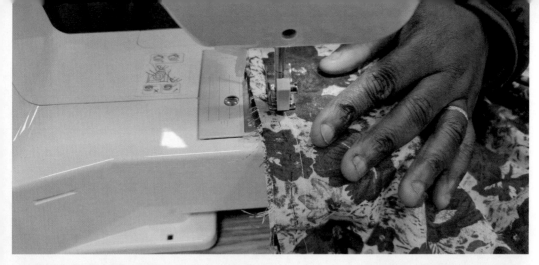

Daniel Charny is also the founder of Fixperts, a learning programme concerned with the role of making in our future lives and how we gain social skills and emotional intelligence through making. 'Most people don't make, it's a massive problem.'[33] Fixperts works through a system of micro-volunteering and constant problem solving. They go out into the community to meet their new partners and empathise with their problem in order to empower them, inviting them to think through making, with material knowledge and making full use of prototypes. He is convinced that maker spaces can affect social groups and improve citizenship, as people feel more agency to influence their surroundings.

Old and new technology

Professional craftspeople have experience of materials and making that is hugely valuable. Makers utilise specialist tools, both old and new, and in skilled hands 3D printers or laser cutters are just another tool. A product designer today will have woodwork and metal tools at their disposal, alongside digital machinery such as a CNC mill, merging the old techniques and new technology. Working with digital tools doesn't mean forgetting the old ways of doing things, in fact, it reinforces the value of the old skills while simultaneously updating them and making them more relevant and contemporary.

There is also an argument that creating software and writing code is in itself a skilled craft, though what you think about that may depend on your age. In *Abstracting Craft: The Practiced Digital Hand*, Malcolm McCullough writes, 'If previously it was usual to assume that computation would only worsen the hand-mind splits engendered by industrialism, now we might reconsider this problem. We might also note the invention of technologies that support the subtleties of the hand.' Back in 1997 he wrote about the fast development of haptic technologies and how they would eventually be of benefit to the small producer and crafts people, enabling them to be more economically viable and removing some of the more repetitive procedures and laborious tasks.

Enterprise and engagement

Critics argue that the Arts and Crafts movement failed in its aims and became a bunch of upper-class intellectuals and aesthetes longing for simpler times. Nostalgia can be a distraction – the challenge for the maker movement is to be democratic and inclusive, not elitist.

The maker movement offers a culture of making that is inclusive, contextual and non-prescriptive. Organisations such as the Maker Assembly are asking who benefits from making? Who is marginalised and who is excluded?

Materials researcher Liz Corbin said [34] of the value of maker spaces, 'Making is hard, alongside others we can challenge our biases,

test our assumptions so inclusivity is core. Making is meaningful in relation to how many people participate.'

The new Arts and Crafts, DIY or maker movement positively encourages enterprise, as evidenced by the growth of regional craft fairs alongside Etsy, Folksy and online sales sites. For young people, the experience of making will increase their life chances and employability, entrepreneurship and skills for the workplace. Giving people a space where they can make is not only educational but may open career options, and raising the profile of the handmade is a great way to encourage young people to make, study and achieve within the creative industries. Young people can be encouraged to pitch products for a museum shop and be given pop-up or online exhibiting and selling space to give them more 'real-world' experience.

Creative practice in schools is now so limited that some may only ever take part in the most basic, 'mess-free' activities, such as cutting and sticking. It is imperative that young people are introduced to materials – wood, fibre, clay, metal – and allowed time to explore their potential.

The Institute of Making, at University College London, is interested in the chemical make-up of the stuff of our world, the intimate matter that was once the preserve of the craftsman who spent many hours becoming acquainted with their raw materials and creating a library of materials as well as a maker space for others to come and tinker. As Zoe Laughlin, materials engineer and director of the cross-curricular Institute of Making, puts it, 'we are all experts at touching stuff, the learning comes from experience.'

The Bauhaus

'We accept the challenge of technical progress with its recognition of social responsibility.'
László Moholy-Nagy

Founded by Walter Gropius in 1919, the Bauhaus Dessau school of art was an experiment in creative education. Although influenced by the Arts and Crafts Movement in its emulation of the craft guild structure, the school had the ambition to unite industry and the arts, rather than separate them. Bauhaus members sought to find creative solutions to society by removing the boundaries between art, design, craft and architecture. They also believed that by embracing new technologies and production techniques, design would become more available and less elitist.

Gropius[35] asked: *'How will we live, how will we settle, what form of community do we want to aspire to?'* So instead of having a hierarchy, they created a community, the idea being that the students would learn not just for the school, or for the sake of it, but for life.

All Bauhaus students completed a preliminary course before specialising in materials such as glass, textiles or clay. Topics covered by this first course included chiaroscuro (the study of light and dark), colour theory and the theory and practice of forms and rhythm – all with a focus on materials.[36] This way of teaching went on to influence the creation of art foundation courses in the UK, as well as in other prominent art colleges across the world. The reliance on craft techniques during the design process was also a precursor of the prototype in designing for industry. In the Manifesto of the Bauhaus, 1919, Gropius wrote, *'Architects, painters, sculptors, we must all return to the crafts! … a base in craft is essential to every artist. It is there that the original source of creativity lies.'*[37]

After the Nazis closed the school in 1933, key members dispersed, creating ripples of the Bauhaus effect across the globe. Gropius and Marcel Breuer moved first to the Isokon, London. Josef and Anni Albers went to Black Mountain College, North Carolina, and then Yale, László Moholy-Nagy to The New Bauhaus American School of Design, Chicago, and Walter Gropius to Harvard's Graduate School of Design.

Their educational theories, as well as the modernist designs they created, have had a lasting legacy.

story
Practical Participation

Everyone's Warehouse in the London borough of Barking and Dagenham is one of the biggest shared, open-access workshops in the UK. Free to use for local residents, the 3,000- square-metre building houses workshops and machinery for woodwork, digital design, ceramics, recycled plastics, fashion and fabrics, as well as an industrial kitchen, an urban garden and spaces for co-working and learning.

Set up in the spring of 2019, Everyone's Warehouse is one element of the broader 'Every One Every Day' project, which was designed and delivered by Participatory City Foundation. Every One Every Day involves thousands of residents working together on neighbourhood projects, ranging from making and fixing to growing, cooking and trading, with the aim of making everyday life better for everyone.

'The idea of Every One Every Day first began about ten years ago,' explains the project's Head of Programmes, Iris Schönherr. 'The founder of Participatory City Foundation, Tessy Britton, spent a decade visiting projects all over the UK, as well as overseas, trying to codify what the things are that encourage people to

connect, participate and get involved with activities in their local area. She manifested that research into a methodology and then secured funding for a live test into whether or not it worked. The first test, "Open Works", was a small prototype involving one team in one space, and from that Tessy made the case for a large-scale prototype with multiple spaces across one whole borough that has become Every One Every Day.'

Every One Every Day is not a volunteering programme, it is about neighbourhoods made by everyone, for everyone, on an equal footing. The majority of the project's work is focused on five Neighbourhood Participation Spaces – or what have become known as 'Neighbourhood Shops' – which are located on high streets across the borough. Open, inclusive and accessible, these are spaces where residents can just pop in to have a cup of tea, access basic making equipment such as sewing machines and simple woodwork tools, and share their local project and business ideas with others. Every One Every Day project designers are also available to help bring ideas to life.

Since the first shop opened in November 2017, Every One Every Day has supported thousands of residents in hundreds of neighbourhood projects. The fact that these projects are rooted in making and doing is crucial to their success. 'If you can get people who may have completely different opinions, making something together, whether that's food or candles or a garden, they very soon forget their differences and start experiencing each other in a positive way, on an equal footing,' says Hayley Bruford, Head of Learning.

As well as these community projects, Every One Every Day also offers Collaborative Business Programmes where people can come together at Everyone's Warehouse to learn new skills and make products, which they go on to sell. 'We're providing something that doesn't usually exist in the eco-system of employment skills or entrepreneurship start-ups,' Iris says. 'We're working with people who wouldn't necessarily seek out existing groups and support, but because our programmes are inclusive, collaborative and pose low personal risk, they are willing to come and give things a try. Barking and Dagenham is a really diverse area, so all sorts of people come. Every One Every Day has designed programmes around many skills such as ceramics, woodwork, food production, clothing and childcare programmes with people aged from 20 to 60, and residents often come with their children.'

Over 40 Collaborative Business Programmes with over 400 sign-ups from residents took place between 2018 and 2022, including initiatives to incubate Grounded, a co-operative coffee shop, and The Good House, which sold essential, circular products designed and made by local people. The economic benefit, while to be welcomed, was, Iris says, 'only one part of what we are testing. The main outcomes we are looking for are around bonding and bridging social capital, skills, confidence, connection and how these play together within a community.'

Every One Every Day's 'Tool To Act' report from 2019 suggests that those outcomes are being achieved. People talked about how using Everyone's Warehouse, taking part in the programmes and visiting the neighbourhood shops helped them to connect with local people and boosted their confidence.

Ags and Kam are two residents of Barking and Dagenham who got involved with the Every One Every Day project and use Everyone's Warehouse. These are their stories:

Ags

'I think I have always been a maker, I'd just forgotten. Years ago, I did some photography and sculpture but then I stopped – you know how life goes. When Everyone's Warehouse opened next to the estate I was living on, I went in with my children and another local mum to see what was going on. They had a kids' room upstairs and we started using the space as a kind of after-school creative

community centre, but I was really inspired by how much else was going on there.

When I discovered the sewing machines in the textile studio I knew I had to try it for myself. The first thing I made was an upcycled chair. All the materials and equipment were there and there was always someone to ask for help and advice. I made new cushions, sanded and painted the frame and gave it to a friend as a housewarming gift. Then I joined a wax-making programme, which was a great experience.

I've moved away from the area now, but I am still making. I'm painting on textiles and I've just had an exhibition. I'm also making candles and exploring eco printing – all these things are using skills I learned at Everyone's Warehouse.

I would probably have discovered making again at some point, but finding Everyone's Warehouse was incredible. Having all the equipment and materials available started me off on the making journey, but the most important thing was the people. Wherever you were working, you could look through a window into another space and see someone doing ceramics, or screen printing, or making something with wood. I found that really inspiring. And there were people there to teach me so many new skills – I'm quite old school but I learned to use some computer programmes and how to use a laser cutter.

Being part of Everyone's Warehouse helped my mental health too. I have an auto-immune disease and I get very depressed at times. I found that making things and doing something with my hands freed me to connect with people and helped me to express those feelings. I've become really interested in the impact that making can have on our wellbeing since I moved. There are a lot of older people where I live now and I am thinking about setting up a community weaving project with them.'

Kam

I studied Surface Design at the London College of Communication, so I was already a maker before I found Everyone's Warehouse. I was working part time in the creative industry and making laser-cut jewellery to sell, but that felt like a side hobby rather than my career. I was using various different maker spaces around London, which were expensive and hard to get to, so I was making slow progress as a designer-maker.

I found Everyone's Warehouse through word of mouth and I couldn't believe it when I arrived – everything I needed, and more, was there under one roof, local to me and free to use. It was full of like-minded, creative people, too.

There was so much going on. I tried out lots of things I wouldn't have otherwise been exposed to, like ceramics and wax making, and I learned 3D printing. I'd always been curious about 3D printing but I'd found the tech intimidating. It was different at Everyone's Warehouse, because skills exchange is a big part of what happens there.

When things began to open up again after the pandemic, Everyone's Warehouse was still quiet, so I spent a lot of time using the laser cutter, experimenting with different designs, textures and materials. Since then I've been selling my jewellery online and I have even had the confidence to take part in a trade fair. I am now a professional maker, and I don't think that would have happened without Everyone's Warehouse.

I have made lots of new friends too. I was considering joining a local sports club, but something like that has much more of a focus. Here you don't know who is going turn up because people come for all sorts of different reasons. It doesn't matter whether you're highly skilled, a complete beginner or just come to have a cup of tea and a chat. It's just nice to be in a creative space with people who live in the same community.

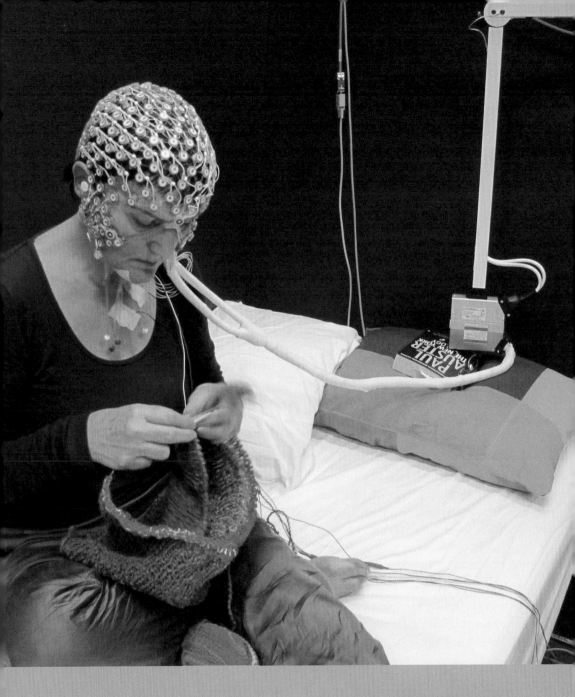

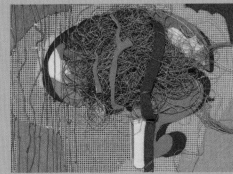

Stitched brain by
Nora Hooijer

Image of the author at the Netherlands Institute for Neuroscience wired up and knitting for EEG registrations
photo: Dr. J. Ramautar

Stitch Your Brain

Artist and former medical doctor Monika Auch has been researching questions around making, such as can creativity be measured? What are the effects of tactile deprivation? Does making help us to create new brain connections?

Stitch Your Brain is a long-term study mapping the hand-brain axis in the context of creativity, with participants asked to embroider their own brains and respond to in-depth questions. The results describe and support the positive influence of crafting for mental wellbeing, for short- and long-term learning, for increased dexterity and for personal empowerment. In her essay *The Intelligence of the Hand,* [38] she says: 'practising as a medical doctor and as an artist needed the same hands-on skills, inquisitiveness and problem-solving approach.'

Her latest book, *Stitch Your Brain*, reflects the results of the empirical study that Auch worked on for a decade from 2013 to 2023. It argues for the importance of creating with your hands in the digital age and documents the positive effects of slow making on neurocognitive learning and on our wellbeing.

The Amsterdam Brainshow, 2018 photo: M. Auch

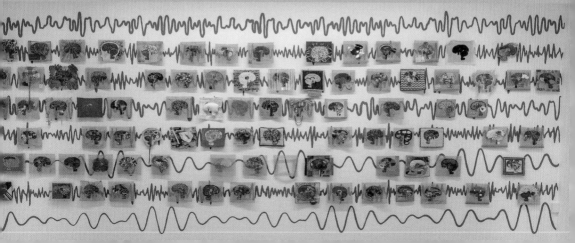

story
Inventor in Residence

 In 2006, a charity was founded in the UK with the vision of supporting exceptionally creative young people. Named Ignite!, this charity now works to unleash that exceptional creativity inside every young person, from toddlers to people in their twenties, through cross-sector programmes and projects in Britain and internationally. Designed to be a bridge between young people, their communities and professional sectors, the central thread running through all Ignite! programmes and projects is giving young people the opportunity to discover more about themselves, raise their confidence, and have their ideas heard and supported.

One of those projects is Lab_13, a family of laboratories based within primary and secondary schools across the UK, America and Africa, which grew out of a similar project in Scotland called 'Room 13'. Dr Bryson Gore was Inventor/Scientist in Residence at Dovecote Primary School in Nottingham, where the first Lab_13 launched, for seven years. This is his story.

Bryson

I joined Lab_13 at Dovecote in 2009. The school is on a huge housing estate (it was the largest in Europe at that time) within sight of Nottingham Trent University. I remember the head teacher saying that the kids' highest aspiration was to work there as a cleaner and that lack of aspiration was what he was trying to change through initiatives such as Lab_13.

I have a background in youth-run youth groups, so the thing that really attracted me to the project was that the Labs are run by a management team made up of students. They are responsible for all aspects of managing the Lab, including recruiting a 'person-in-residence' with either a scientific, engineering or inventing background to help with investigations, lend a hand with experiments where needed and ensure everything is done safely.

I did 'Goo' – mixing up flour and water – for my interview. It's a pretty classic primary school experiment because it's fun and

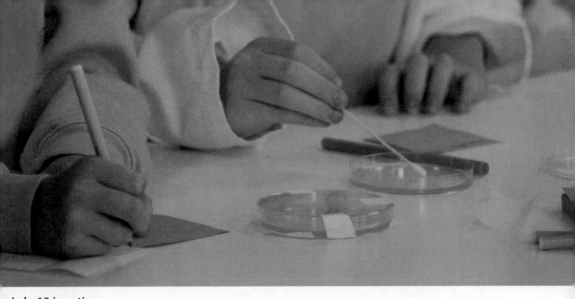

Lab_13 in action,

weird, but there's an extra feature you can add where if you put the mixture into a really big loudspeaker and power it with the right frequency of sound, it turns into a quivering, creature-like blob that sends out tendrils and climbs and crawls. Kids find it absolutely fascinating. I included it because it's a great example of how you can stimulate children to ask questions with incredibly simple things. And once they're asking questions, you're away, you don't need to teach, you just need to help them investigate.

I spent two days each week in school as part of the normal day, and I ran a lunchtime club too. I wasn't curriculum-based; class teachers allocated a period a week for the Lab and sent me small groups of kids. When I started, I tended to be funded through the 'gifted and talented' scheme, but then there was a shift to the Pupil Premium, which focused on children from disadvantaged backgrounds. Under both models, it wasn't uncommon for me to have kids who found being in the classroom a bit difficult.

That difficulty was often driven by them not seeing the point of what they were learning. The key difference with Lab_13 was that it wasn't about telling the students what to do. As Inventor in Residence, my role was to help them express what they were interested in and make that come alive. Very often, especially with the boys, when I asked them what they were interested in, it turned out that they were utterly preoccupied with something and we were able to explore that. One of the kids, for example, was really interested in tornado chasers in the United States, so we decided to build a tornado machine. He came to the Lab every week, and when

89

it was ready, he presented it to the entire school. That achievement was entirely driven by his interest. He learned to focus, to make, and then had the confidence to talk about what he had made to 200 of his peers.

Another project I did with all the kids who came to the Lab was to teach them to solder. Traditionally, soldering in science is all about making electrical currents, which is totally irrelevant to the kids. But they did find it almost unbelievable that a metal could turn into a liquid and back again. I taught them that they could glue wires together, which they thought was fascinating because they were impossible to break, and a lot of them just liked melting blobs of solder into spheres, or using the spheres to make jewellery, or animals. They were enthralled by the realisation that they could fabricate something they wanted and then they would ask, 'how do I make more things like that?' That is a tremendous driver for motivating children into a process of discovery.

The other great thing about soldering is that it is notoriously something that requires a minimum of three hands – you have to hold the soldering iron, the solder and the object you are wanting to apply solder to. That requires an incredible level of dexterity. If you give a child a soldering iron, nine times out of ten they'll pick it up in a way that makes it really difficult to use, so you tell them to hold it like a pencil and then they get it. Seventy-five per cent of the kids at Dovecote Primary left being able to solder.

In my opinion, the practical value of learning to use a soldering iron is relevant to very few. The reason I taught the kids at Dovecote to do it was to demonstrate the validity of pursuing what they found interesting and to show them that they have the ability to shape their environment. That is utterly empowering. I also wanted them to realise that physically engaging with something is an excellent way to work things out. As AI blows out of the water the educational requirement that children know facts, being able to work something out is going to become increasingly important.

Lab_13 in action,

photo: courtesy of Ignitefutures.org.uk

The Leader of the Luddites, satirical print, published by E. Walker, 1812

The world of AI

'The principal goal of education is to create men who are capable of doing new things, not simply of repeating what other generations have done – men who are creative, inventive, and discoverers. The second goal of education is to form minds which can be critical, can verify, and not accept everything they are offered.'
Jean Piaget[39]

There is much discussion about the rise of artificial intelligence (AI) and the threat of an end to civilisation as we know it. As with previous revolutions, there is a fear of the unknown and calls for regulation before society experiences some kind of *Bladerunner*, sentient-robots-take-over-the-world scenario. There is going to be change and we hope we will have a generation of young people who can recognise AI-generated material for what it is and respond accordingly. Used ethically, AI may be a tool for democratising work if there is open source access. As with the invention of other dubiously received devices, such as the spinning jenny, mechanised weaving looms and the traction engine, people will want to throw spanners in the works in a Luddite manner. In fact, contrary to common belief, the Luddites were not anti-machine, just underpaid and in fear of losing their livelihoods.

In terms of art education, AI bots such as ChatGPT may be able to offer students information, perhaps lists of the labels of art theories. The machine learning, that draws information from what it has read before, is a one-dimensional tool. This will be disembodied knowledge, some formal and possibly inaccurate facts, not the rich knowledge that comes from learning through the senses. However, we may be able to control it as a tool to do more than just change the channel on our smart speaker while our hands are busy doing something more important. All the more reason to roll up your sleeves and get your hands dirty.

Based at the British Library, London, The Alan Turing Institute has set up an AI and arts interest group to look at the impact that AI may have on our cultural heritage, the creative industries and policy makers in areas such as digitising collections and text recognition. Their cross-disciplinary research also recognises AI as a creative tool as well as the role that art has to play in helping us to understand and critique the ethics of AI.

Part Three

Wellbeing + Activism

Occupational Therapy

'A messy head can be liberated by the ritual of knitting mindfully.'

Rachael Matthews, *The Mindfulness in Knitting*

The use of craft as therapy is not new to this century. Nurses and community workers instinctively knew that it was worthwhile to give people a purpose – something useful to do with their hands and their minds – though there may be more to it than that.

Basket cases

What do you think of when you hear the term 'basket case'? It's a pejorative term that is used today to denote someone of extreme nervousness. It might come from the basket-chairs used by invalids – but the origin of the phrase is unclear. Perhaps, one possible source is the use of basketry, along with other crafts, during the Boer War as occupational therapy (OT) for soldiers recovering in hospitals from their wartime wounds, both physical and psychological. Modern language has changed, for the main part, and we now have more respectful terminology for mental health and disability. However, the principles behind the phrase remain the same: the process of making

something by hand provides physical and mental therapy. We have records of soldiers being taught knitting and basketry in hospitals, using peg looms to accommodate difficulties such as the loss of a hand or arm. As well as being an activity that passed the time, the process of making allowed the brain to learn something new and distracted the invalided soldiers from disturbing and intrusive thoughts and pain.

Crafting as therapy has come in and out of fashion. Historically, Occupational Health practitioners didn't like to be seen as 'handicraft' teachers; their role, they argued, was not to fill the hours that a recuperating patient might have to fill, but rather to use their extensive knowledge to train the two sides of the brain – the hand and the eye – to work together. Today, OT practitioners stress the need for this therapeutic craft to be mindful, rather than the mindlessness of being on autopilot while doing something repetitive, such as driving. Occupational therapy needs to be active and attentive, rather than passive, therefore capable of eliciting flow.

Metal working at the Cripples' Guild, Hanley photo: Guild of Handicrafts

In their book *Mindful Crafts as Therapy: Engaging More Than Hands*, Cynthia Evetts and Suzanne Peloquin write, 'When engaged in individualized craft interventions, clients make positive shifts in health, becoming crafters with choice while occupied in productive work.'[1] The theory of many experienced OT practitioners is that learning crafts stimulates and develops cognitive function and promotes the orderly processes of thought, and can help us to exert some control over the world, or at least our own lives, and the final product can be a metaphor for the healing process. All activities have a meaning, or cultural baggage, so, as with our jobs, some people will enjoy one and not another. Research shows[2] that we need to match this with how it fits our motor system as well as our personality, in order to feel that flow and purpose (see page 130).

Stoke-on-Trent had its own silverware guild to provide occupation for workers injured in the potteries and also for children to learn the trade through apprenticeships, teaching them to create copper and silverplate, as well as other crafts, such as bookbinding.

Millicent Sutherland Leveson-Gower established the Duchess of Sutherland's Cripples Guild (DSCG), which was originally set up in 1898 as The Potteries and Newcastle Crippled Children's Guild to serve the children of workers at the potteries of Stoke-on-Trent and environs. The Guild produced the finest silverware influenced by Scottish Arts and Crafts style, from a factory in the grounds of her home, Trentham Hall, and then in Wilson Street, Hanley, Stoke-on-Trent. It's unclear whether the poor development of these children was due to

95

Advertisement for
the Duchess of Sutherland's
Guild of Handicrafts

Right: **Bedridden wounded,
knitting.** Walter Reed Hospital,
Washington, DC

photo: Harris & Ewing

neglect by poorly paid working parents, or by
their exposure to lead glazes. Other similarly
named institutions were established in
Leicester, Nottingham and the Isle of Man,
but these seem to have concentrated on
medical treatment rather than rehabilitation.
By 1910 the DSCG had grown to supply a
shop in Bond Street with a clientele that
included Queen Victoria.[3]

A modern-day equivalent to the DSCG might
be the social enterprise Fine Cell Work, who
use the transformative nature of needlework
in prisons. Their team of volunteers teaches
crewel work to prisoners, who can then
receive commissions and earn money for their
work. Their aims include purposeful activity,
opportunity and reintegration. Fine Cell
Work also operate Open the Gates, a
rehabilitation programme, which offers
purpose and advice to those leaving prison.
Reports of the benefits include having a
constructive way to use their time, helping
ex-prisoners to earn money, re-build their
self-esteem and emotional resilience.[4]

Part of the benefit of making is the sense
of purpose inherent in a meaningful activity.
Scholar and author Ellen Dissanayake[5] points
out that we are defined by anthropologists as
Homo Faber, the toolmaking animal, leaving
our mark on the world. 'The care or control
required to fashion and embellish an
important tool was like a metaphor for the
care and control one wished to exercise in
using it and the value one imbued it with,'
she says. She goes on to talk about joie de
faire, or the joy of making, believing we are
denying this to young people.

Arts and crafts are invaluable in making
rituals and ceremonies, such as funerals and
births, impressive, memorable and unique,
including projects such as knitting shawls,
making coffins and decorating tables.
'Because people care about the results,
rituals are not performed casually: words,
voices, actions, movements, bodies,
surroundings and paraphernalia are made as
impressive or scared or beautiful or
extraordinary as they possibly can be.'

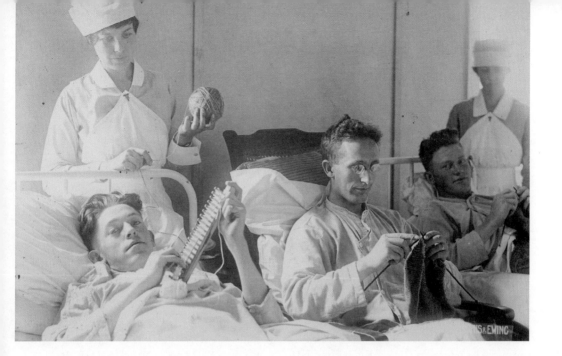

Dissanayake looks at making as a social necessity that we can't thrive without, she believes that 'Someone acquainted with human evolutionary history must question whether our species can prosper if so many of its evolved abilities are not fostered and so many of its evolved needs are not met. Making is not only pleasurable, but meaningful – indeed, it is because it is meaningful that it is pleasurable, like other meaningful things, such as food, friends, rest, sex, babies and children and useful work are pleasurable because they are necessary to our survival as individuals and as a species. A society that devalues making, and making important things special, forfeits a critical component of its members' birthright.'

Community

Anyone who has been to, or run, a craft workshop can tell you that people are not just there for the making. Of course, there are those who solely wish to expand their skills base, but there are more who are there for the social interaction it offers. It works a treat for a talking circle: because people are busy with their hands, they are able to converse more freely. Eyes are averted, looking down at the work, so there is no embarrassing too-long eye contact, and occasional silent pauses are totally acceptable because people are often lost in concentration. This is a well-known effect, also seen when people talk while walking side by side, or travelling in a car, where conversations can often be more intense and revealing.

Another side-effect of making is what is called 'effort-based reward'. This is the payback from your act of creation, where you may receive praise for your work and admiration from others in your social group. You also have the enjoyment of the finished object you have created, or the pleasure of gifting it to someone else, and the warm glow that comes with giving (and hoping they appreciate the work that went into it).

The Arts and Humanities Research Council (AHRC) funded project: Co-Creating CARE: Community Asset-based Research & Enterprise,[6] found that through acts of small citizenship, creative making can be powerfully, if quietly, activist. Unlike more familiar crafts activism, such "acts" are not limited to overtly political and public manifestations of social action, but rather concern the micro-politics of the individual, the grass roots community and the social every day. The project used the work of the craft circle to explore the benefits of amateur crafters working together, such as building capacities for resilience, critical thinking and confidence to operate in the world and exploring the concept of 'community' beyond our immediate neighbourhood, to include communities of practice and online communities. This shows the value of the sewing bee or knitting group and why such collaborative crafts have persisted.

Wellbeing

In November 2018 the then new Health Secretary Matt Hancock gave a speech[7] to the King's Fund extolling the power of the arts to improve lives and advocating the increased use of 'life-enhancing' social prescribing. 'We know what the NHS does is life-saving. But what the arts and social activities do is life-enhancing. You might get by in a world without the arts, but it isn't a world that any of us would choose to live in.'

If you were being cynical you might think this is just a tactic to save money, by diverting resources into other areas. 'It's scientifically proven,' he said. 'Access to the arts and social activities improves people's mental and physical health. It makes us happier and healthier.'

A literature review, commissioned by Arts Council England, entitled 'Arts, Culture & the Brain',[8] shows that arts participation benefits wellbeing in all sorts of groups. It states: 'There is also extensive evidence that arts engagement is associated with changes in psychological capabilities and motivational processes in children, adolescents, adults, and older adults, ranging from the development of behaviour to cognitive decline.' However, the review found less evidence in existing research on the association between neurophysiology and taking part in arts, with most physical examples concentrating on movement and dance, which has been found to benefit spectators as well as participants.

We know that there are many reasons why taking part can improve health and wellbeing and these are just a few:

- Effort-based reward
- Flow and lack of self-consciousness
- Social cohesion
- Thoughtfulness
- Agency

The power of stitch

Former physiotherapist Betsan Corkhill advocates for the use of therapeutic knitting as a healthcare tool through Stitchlinks, the non-profit community interest company she founded in 2005, and the EWE Foundation, a philanthropic organisation established in Cyprus, in 2019, that aims to better co-ordinate the many associations and groups interested in developing a circular economy of wool across Europe.

Therapeutic knitting, like ordinary knitting, involves wool, needles and two active hands, but what makes it distinct is the thinking behind the activity. Betsan developed this term and describes it as 'a combination of knitting and knowledge'; the knowledge being an understanding of how to enhance the benefits of knitting to deliberately improve wellbeing and, for those who live with a medical condition, learning about that condition and how knitting can help to manage and alleviate symptoms.

Betsan Corkhill, Sarah Corbett and others taking part in the Craftivists Garden, 2014

photo: Craftivist Collective

In 2010 Stitchlinks produced a survey with Cardiff University to discover how knitting affected the mental and social wellbeing of individuals. There were lots of questions, over 50 in fact, and the compilers were concerned that they wouldn't get enough completed surveys back. They needn't have worried: the knitting networks worked their magic and they received 3,514 valid

responses in two weeks from 31 different countries. When asked why they knitted, one of the most common answers from respondents was 'for relaxation'. The other reasons were being productive while engaging in other more passive activities, such as watching TV, travelling or waiting, creating social connections and having a creative outlet. The majority said that knitting improved their mood, with 81 per cent of respondents claiming that knitting made them feel happier.

Betsan Corkhill, Knit for Health and Wellness, FlatBear Publishing, 2014

So surely everyone should be encouraged to take part? Activity groups that give people purpose and enjoyment could save a huge amount of money for the NHS and a knitting group can fit in well with a clinical unit as a low-risk and low-cost solution, but because it is so hard to definitively prove the benefits, real long-term funding is slow in coming. A knitting group can fit in well with a clinical unit as a low-risk and low-cost solution, and even paying for a group leader would only be for two hours a week – not a huge cost. Clinics are full of people on the maximum doses of anti-depressants and morphine-based drugs for pain relief, and they take up time that clinicians don't have, so there has to be another approach. At the other end of the spectrum a high percentage of people visiting their GP aren't going with a solvable problem, more for a listening ear because they just need someone to talk to. Betsan says, 'A GP's time is taken up with people who could be using a social knitting group in a GP's surgery run by a district nurse, potentially saving the NHS millions of pounds.'

Betsan believes that 'A high number of people are managing long-term pain or post-traumatic stress and don't have access to this kind of activity. There is a huge problem in society in that we have developed a very passive attitude to health care. People who take responsibility for themselves are pro-active and knitting puts the power back into their hands.'

Betsan Corkhill is a strong advocate for the therapeutic power of knitting. This is her story:

Until 2002 I was a senior physiotherapist, working in the community. Many of the patients I saw were so demotivated I knew they wouldn't do the exercises I'd taught them, nor carry out the lifestyle changes I advised – Mrs Smith wasn't getting out of her chair because she had no reason to.

I felt we needed to take a step back with these individuals. Before any self-management approach would be successful, they needed to develop an interest in the world, an aspiration to improve their wellbeing, and an opportunity to enjoy social contact. The system we found ourselves in took no consideration of the whole person and the critical role that psychological wellbeing and 'whole life' events play in the healing process. I became very frustrated.

After much soul searching, I decided on a complete change of career and became a freelance production editor on a range of leisure-based magazines. Two years later, I found myself working on the craft portfolio of Future Publishing, and it was here that I stumbled across a large amount of anecdotal evidence on the therapeutic benefits of knitting and stitching. Large numbers of people from different backgrounds and cultures around the world were telling similar stories of using knitting and stitching to successfully self-manage a variety of medical conditions, in particular stress, depression and long-term pain. I immediately thought of those 'community patients' and decided to investigate further.

I began to think of ways in which I could get the message across to others who might benefit and, in January 2005, I founded Stitchlinks. The idea was to create a central hub that could always be trusted and relied upon to give accurate information.

As I dug down, it soon became clear that the benefits were going much deeper than simply occupying or distracting people. This was something hugely exciting, which had the potential to change not only the way we approach our general wellbeing, but also the management of long-term health conditions.

In 2006, I approached the Royal United Hospital, Bath, with
my findings (I described knitting as a 'bilateral rhythmic social
intervention' to make it more appealing to clinicians and
scientists), and six months later I had an email inviting me
to set up a therapeutic knitting group, linked to the hospital's
pain clinic.

The doctors, or more commonly the Nurse Practitioner, would refer
certain patients to me. They were usually the people with the most
complex physical and mental health problems who weren't
responding to treatment.

Explaining how knitting can help with pain is complex. Our
understanding of pain has changed enormously and it is now
recognised that, for long-term pain, it's more a question of the
pain-making process going awry rather than a problem with
a particular joint, muscle or body part.

The brain's job is to keep us alive, not to keep us happy, so, if
anything, our brains are biased towards looking for threat and
negative things to keep us safe. When there's potential damage
to the body, sensory receptors called 'nociceptors' fire off
electrochemical signals that travel to the spinal cord and up to
the brain, which then, depending on the context, chooses whether
or not to pay attention to that signal. If, having weighed up all
incoming information – including past experiences, present context
and predicted future – the brain decides that there is a threat, you
will then experience pain.

The brain is also continuously sending down information via the
spinal cord. This information has the power to modulate those
incoming signals, either ramping up or turning down the volume.
If a person feels happy, has a good supportive social network
or is meaningfully occupied, those signals will be turned down
and they will experience less pain. Conversely, if a person is
experiencing low mood, is anxious, has depression or is socially

Knitting Tent Women's National Service School, Navy league photo Harris & Ewing, 1916, Library of Congresss

isolated they are more likely to perceive threat, which will ramp up those signals and make it much more likely that they will feel pain.

Many of the people who come to see me can have as many as a dozen different health labels. This is usually because they have been sent down a different health pathway for each of their symptoms, seeing a different 'specialist' for each. My first-hand experience with these people, coupled with my thinking, has led me to look at health and pain from a systems rather than symptoms perspective.

I would argue that pain is an experience that emerges as a result of the complex conversation that is continually taking place between everything going on within our bodies and in the world around us concluding that there is a threat. Environment and context play an important part in this, as do issues such as a person's sleep quality, social interactions, nutrition, levels of physical activity, mood and, perhaps most importantly, their sense of safety.

I am coming more and more to the conclusion that our sense of safety is crucial to our sense of wellbeing and health. When we feel safe, our parasympathetic nervous system – which is our rest, digest and heal system – is turned up. But most people with long-term health issues are stuck in a state of stress where the sympathetic fight, flight or freeze nervous system is dominant. This means the body is unable to recover or heal. Since the body has a natural bias towards wanting to heal itself, surely the first thing we should do is to enable people to feel safe, which is a state that optimises the potential for healing?

There is some recognition now that rhythm, because it's predictable, plays an important role in creating a sense of safety. Knitting is a rhythmic process. I have produced a document listing 25 ways that knitting can help with pain, based on responses from my patients at the therapeutic knitting group and other people who have made their way to Stitchlinks or to see me in my role as a lifestyle health coach.

Knitting group c.1923   photo Harris & Ewing, Library of Congresss

They are:

1 Facilitates mindful meditation.
2 Facilitates relaxation.
3 Distracts – distraction is one of the most effective analgesics we know of.
4 Encourages positive thought cycles to help break negativity.
5 Takes pain away from the forefront of your mind.
6 Takes the focus away from YOU and your pain.
7 Motivates you to try other things.
8 Improves mood and the feelings of depression often associated with pain.
9 Improves feelings of loneliness/isolation, giving a sense of belonging.
10 Helps to manage the stress and worry associated with pain.
11 Teaches patience and perseverance – helps to learn pacing and deal with its frustrations.
12 Lessens the frustrations of enforced rest periods – enables productivity at rest.
13 Helps deal with flare-ups.
14 Raises self-esteem and confidence so you feel better equipped to manage your pain.
15 Improves feelings of self-worth in society, usefulness and contribution.
16 Provides structure and purpose to a day.
17 Improves feelings of control for those who feel controlled by their pain, doctors, drugs.
18 May break cycles of hyper vigilance to pain.
19 Enables you to experience excitement, anticipation and achievement again.
20 Involves you in the world again – opening up your world.

21 You can take knitting anywhere, and portability means you can deal with pain anytime, anywhere.
22 Calms – dealing with the 'Why me?' anger that many feel.
23 Lessens tension.
24 Introduces enjoyment and fun into life, so life becomes more than pain and chores.
25 Encourages you to look forward to tomorrow.

At the moment, we lack the evidence base to back up these ideas, which means there is still very little going on in clinical settings in the UK. But elsewhere things are happening slowly. The President of EWE, Dr Alberto Costa, is a retired Italian breast cancer surgeon who noticed that women who knitted in the waiting room while waiting for appointments and treatments coped better than those who didn't. He contacted me several years ago and, when

Creative workshops

photo: courtesy of The
Creative Dimension Trust

the EWE Foundation was established, 'promoting the use
of indigenous wool in therapeutic knitting, crochet and felting
for health and social programmes' was written into its statutes.
Therapeutic knitting is now taking place in about 42 hospitals
across Italy.

In 2020, a study began in Milan which used a MEG scanner to
identify brain activity and measure small magnetic fields produced
by the brain in 40 people immediately after crocheting. (The study
focused on crochet rather than knitting because it took place during
the pandemic and it was easier to supply sterilised crochet hooks
than knitting needles in a sterile bag.) The group was compared
with a control. At the time of writing, the paper has been submitted
and is now going through the peer review process. If it's accepted,
it will be a big step forward.

The lessons we're learning through all this work have the potential
to change the way the medical profession (and, importantly, those
in management) view and treat individuals with long-term health
conditions. It also highlights the need for us all to take responsibility
for and control of our own wellbeing, because there's a lot we can
do as individuals to improve whatever situation we find ourselves
in. We may not be far away from the time when doctors routinely
advise patients to take a dose of knitting twice a day.

The European Twiddle Muff Awards organised by OZANA and the European Wool Exchange Foundation, at the University Psychiatric Hospital Vrapče, Zagreb, Croatia photo: Lenard Stipkovic

Sensory stimulation and dementia

A Twiddle Muff is exactly what it sounds like – a fabric tube or muffler with buttons and other textures sewn into it that is designed to be twiddled with. This sensory tool was designed by Margaret Light in 1997 after she observed her grandmother, a dementia patient, fiddling with her hands. It might be sewn, knitted or crocheted and contain different textures, with loops and accessories sewn on, but nothing that might present a choking hazard.

Many patients may be deprived of physical touch and other incidental haptic contact that people might expect to have in an average day. They are also good for keeping hands warm if there is poor circulation, which is often an issue for elderly people who are leading a sedentary life. The group Handmade for Dementia[9] has developed a Dementia Cannula Sleeve, which has the additional benefit of covering up the cannula entry points and other medical tubes that may be fiddled with and dislodged or become painful if there is nothing else available to play with. The sleeves were trialled for two months at a Chester hospital

towards the end of 2017 and were so successful that an army of volunteers were recruited to make more. 'Knitting helps people help others. We're all doing our bit,' says founder Sharon Wallace Holdstock.

Cathy Treadaway, Professor of Creative Practice at Cardiff Metropolitan University, is the Principal Investigator of LAUGH (Ludic Artefacts Using Gesture and Haptics) project, which has co-designed playful objects for people with dementia to help them achieve 'in the moment' living. 'In the advanced stages of the disease people can become very withdrawn and have great difficulty in communicating with their loved ones and with carers,'[10] she explains. Their research has found that sensory stimulation can reduce anxiety and agitation. Digital technology has been used to create haptic feedback, such as a 'heartbeat' for a cuddly toy to hug and a vibrating steering wheel, providing augmented touch sensation. The project has found that hand stimulation improves wellbeing and improved communication from participants.

story
Healing

Dubbed the 'godmother of craftivism' by a Greek newspaper back in the first decade of the twenty-first century, US-based Betsy Greer has spent much of her adult life investigating how making things with our hands can improve our own lives, the lives of the people in our communities, and the world at large. Her books include *Knitting for Good* (Roost Books) and *Craftivism: The Art of Craft and Activism* (Arsenal Pulp Press), and she is the creative force behind the stitch-focused community projects Dear Textiles and You Are So Very Beautiful. This is her story.

My understanding that you could use craft to create the world you wanted to see grew from talking to my grandmother. She knitted hats for newborns in the hospital she volunteered at, and although she would have never called herself an activist, boy did she make the world better with her own two hands. Quietly. Deftly. In objects that were given to babies born to relatives and strangers and community members.

She taught me cross stitch when I was a child. She could be stern, but when it came to crafts, my grandmother was all about the love that they provide. I sat in my grandfather's big leather chair and fumbled with the tiny stitches, making a bookmark design I had picked out for my mother at the craft store.

I stitched a few things here and there through my teenage years, but I didn't really pick up craft again until I was living in New York City in my twenties. I found something sacred in the softness of the yarn and the click of the needle, even though my first scarf was crooked and full of holes. I found that there was a sense of power in the making of something from nothing. That's when I began to really think about the ways in which people create change and first made the connection between craft and activism. I looked at how people were protesting various issues and at how craftivism

Betsy Greer knitting

photo: Josh Sosin

had been used in England during the Second World War, then in multiple wars in multiple countries, as a way for people to use their interests and skills to share their voices and to create change.

Between 2003 and 2004 I was studying for an MA in sociology at Goldsmiths, University of London, and writing a dissertation on knitting, DIY culture and community development. I often knitted in public – on the tube, waiting for the bus – and people were always coming up to me, talking to me, and telling me their stories. I realised that knitting provided this incredible way to connect with people regardless of whether you speak the same language, are of the same generation or have the same economic or cultural background. The fact that you are making something breaks down barriers and that allows for an openness.

Then, around 2014, I started delving into my own history of personal trauma, which led to the realisation that I had repressed memories of being attacked. All of a sudden, it made sense that I was so interested in digging into how people could use their voices, because I had silenced mine for 18 years. That discovery has led me to explore projects around agency and resilience and the transformation that not just knitting, but all textile-based work can bring.

I know from my own experience how people silence themselves and also how they can heal and connect through craft. When I tried making daily affirmations using a five-minute journal app, I found coming up with a positive statement about myself every day was literally the hardest task of my morning. Affirmations can be healing, but if the words don't ring true, they can draw attention to a negative thought instead. I didn't believe the affirmation 'I am so very beautiful' about myself. Often, I found myself saying the affirmation, 'you are so very beautiful' and it felt like a mistake. So I thought, what if I stitch the affirmations? Because stitching is a slow process and I was interested in what would soak in as I looked at the words I was stitching over time. It worked.

Betsy Greer, You Are So Very Beautiful workshop
North Carolina Museum of Art   photo: Rachel Berbec

Craft can be a good conduit to being present. As well as being present in the actual process of making, you can also see how time, how the present, has passed in the thing you are making. Even if you do no more than a single row of knitting each day, each of those rows provides physical evidence that time has passed and that you are growing and healing.

Creating something also means making choices – what colour will it be, what yarn will you use? The choices involved in making are an element of agency. If you are feeling that things are out of control, looking at something you have made and the choices it involved can be a talisman of strength.

For me, craftivism is as much about fighting the bad things we tell ourselves as it is about fighting the bad things of this world. It is about healing ourselves as we make, and then maybe healing the world with the things we produce.

Touch

Professor Francis McGlone of John Moores University, Liverpool, has been doing research into touch, which he sees as an undervalued sense, indeed, not just a sentimental human indulgence, but a biological necessity. Although as a society we are more connected in some ways, we have less everyday touch than ever before.

Professor McGlone argues that touch plays a fundamental role in the way the human brain develops, and that a lack of it can be detrimental. The nurturing touch that would normally develop between a mother and infant and then go on through daily contact, is a gentle touch that is part of human development. A lack of touch was infamously seen in the children in Romanian orphanages discovered at the fall of the Ceaușescu regime in 1989. Even the infants that had been fed and watered were not given any human contact, and all of the children grew up with severe behavioural and developmental problems. This is the kind of touch that is crucial for reducing stress, maintaining personal connections and intimacy, and is good for our mental health. It's thought that people who do not receive enough rewarding, affectionate touch as they grow up may seek to replace that reward with other stimuli, such as food, drugs or alcohol.

The other kind of touch that we normally think of is fast touch, almost instantaneous touch –

such as that of a hot flame or a sharp object. These sensory nerves are all over the body, concentrated in the glabrous, or hairless, skin of the hands and also in the feet and mouth. The feedback travels to the brain more quickly than through other senses, and in some people these sensors can become more acute. So, for instance, a blind person reading braille may be able to read more quickly than someone reading visually.

These nerves are also crucial for proprioception, our sense of our body's position in space, so if you are without the sense of touch you cannot easily perform normal functions. In Anni Albers' 1938 essay 'Work with Material', for the Black Mountain College bulletin, she claimed: 'we must come down to earth from the clouds where we live in vagueness and experience the most real thing there is: material.'

In her book *On Weaving*, published in 1965, she writes about material tactility and how there is too much talking and not enough touching, bemoaning the nature of modern day life.

Albers explains:
'We touch things to assure ourselves of reality. We touch the objects of our love. We touch the things we form. Our tactile experiences are elemental. If we reduce their range, as we do when we reduce the necessity to form things ourselves, we grow

Opposite: Sabel Saddlery
Right: Savoir Beds

photos: Carmel King

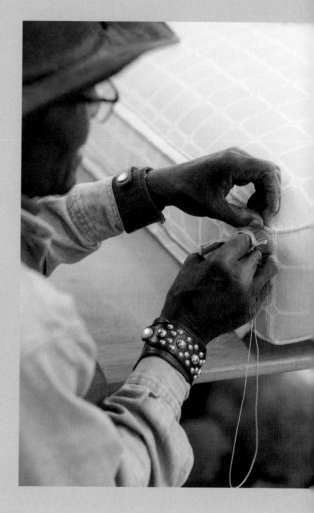

lopsided. We are apt today to overcharge our grey matter with words and pictures – that is, with material already transposed into a certain key, pre-formulated material, and to fall short in providing for a stimulus that may touch off our creative impulse, such as unformed material, material "in the rough".'

She describes the aesthetic sensibility required to *discern matière* – material, matter or the surface quality of things – as separate from the intellectual structure of things, though we need both to work together.

'Structure, as related to function, needs our intellect to construct it or, analytically, to decipher it. Matière, on the other hand, is mainly non-functional, non-utilitarian, and in that respect, like colour, it cannot be experienced intellectually. It has to be approached, just like colour, non-analytically, receptively. It asks to be enjoyed and valued for no other reason than its intriguing performance of a play of surfaces. But it takes sensibility to respond to matière, as it does to respond to colour. Just as only a trained eye and a receptive mind are able to discover meaning in the language of colours, so it takes these and in addition an acute sensitivity to tactile articulation to discover meaning in that of matière. Thus the task today is to train this sensitivity in order to regain a faculty that once was so naturally ours.'[11]

Idle hands

'Hoot' the mother of two young boys used to cry. Code for 'hands out of trousers', it was a coded plea for them to stop fiddling with themselves when other people were there. Boys have often been encouraged to keep their hands out of their pockets, lest they entertain their personal body parts too much. This distancing of the body is similar for young ladies, who were encouraged to keep their hands otherwise occupied so that they would not be tempted to engage in anything that might be perceived as improper. Hands were kept still in churches through the Germanic practice of joining hands in prayer, where they could be clearly seen.

The psychology of the transitional object was explored at depth by the English paediatrician and psychoanalyst Donald Winnicott[12] in his observations of infant development. We generally think of this as being a comfort blanket or cuddly toy that can help a baby or toddler to separate from their mother when falling asleep alone. Occasionally you may see an adult holding a soft toy or doll in the same way, which looks incongruous, so we tend to have transitional objects that are age-appropriate, such as a pen or handbag. In his book, *Hands*, Darian Leader[13] points out that rosary beads or cigarettes were most common, and now it seems fidget gadgets or smartphones are the new acceptable accessory. If you are in a socially awkward situation, eating alone or waiting for someone in a cafe, you may find yourself reaching for something to busy yourself with – a book, newspaper, your phone. Having that third item to focus our attention on gives us a sense of purpose and relieves us from feeling out of place.

Fidgeting in the classroom can also be due to poor core strength[14] and has been noted by outdoor play specialists who say being outside in nature is one of the best antidotes to sitting at a desk. The combination of nature and exercise is one that is beneficial to all of us. For children, running on uneven ground and playing with natural materials can only strengthen their sense of balance, both physically and materially. Angela Hanscom is a paediatric occupational therapist with a degree in kinesiology. She set up TimberNook to promote active free play for kids, especially out of doors, as a counter to the passive screen entertainment they are led to consume. In her professional capacity she began seeing increasing numbers of children who had sensory problems, poor balance, and concern from the school that they 'couldn't sit still'. Children with poor strength and grip who may not be able to hang on to a rope may not be able to grasp a pencil either. A lack of motor stability has the effect of not being able to sit still, or constant fidgeting. 'Children are going to class with bodies that are less prepared to learn than ever before. With sensory systems not quite working right, they are asked to sit and pay attention. Children naturally start

fidgeting in order to get the movement their body so desperately needs and is not getting enough of to "turn their brain on." What happens when the children start fidgeting? We ask them to sit still and pay attention; therefore, their brain goes back to sleep.'

Hanscom goes on to say, 'Fidgeting is a real problem. It is a strong indicator that children are not getting enough movement throughout the day.' This constant wriggling and moving around of children in a classroom may be a distraction but it may also be a way of the

body exercising itself. Dr Kat Arney, in her podcast *Fidget on Four* on BBC Radio 4, says that rather than needing to sit quietly when we are learning, for some people fidgeting can aid concentration and help us to focus.

People can often be observed doodling in meetings, or taking over-extensive notes to keep themselves engaged. Knitting, crochet and sewing can also be seen in long meetings and conferences. Far from being a sign of disinterest, it can help to keep the brain on task while the hands are occupied.

Sometimes fidgeting can aid decision-making. Anne Churchland is Chair of Cold Spring Harbor Neuroscience, New York, and studies the neural mechanisms of decision-making. Her research with mice shows that they make movements when they are learning or making decisions, and demonstrates how movement and neural activity is not just related[15] but that physical movements can profoundly shape neural activity. The studies looked at movements and brain activity that were not directly related to the task in hand, but how those extraneous movements might be involved in the overall process. 'The profound impact of uninstructed movements on neural activity suggests that movement signals play a critical role in cortical information processing. Widespread integration of movement signals might be advantageous for sensory processing, cancelling of self-motion, gating of inputs [controlling what your senses absorb] or permitting distributed associational learning. All of these functions build on the idea that the brain creates internal models of the world that are based on the integration of sensory and motor information to predict future events.'[16]

Anna Freud, daughter of Sigmund and a pioneer of child psychoanalysis as well as a keen weaver, famously knitted while listening to her patients and had a whole floor loom in her consulting room. The slow and rhythmic activity of weaving allows your mind to wander and be filled with thoughts, much like dreaming or the 'free association' that Sigmund Freud asked of his patients in therapeutic sessions. Anna Freud, it is said, composed her psychoanalytic papers while working on her loom, and one still resides at the Freud Museum in London.[17]

Some of our best ideas can come about when we are weaving, doing the washing up or weeding in the garden. Researchers have found[18] that engaging in simple external tasks that allow the mind to wander may facilitate creative problem solving.

A deficit of attention

The rising rates of diagnosis for Attention Deficit and Hyperactivity Disorder (ADHD) have been noted for many years, notably by the late Sir Ken Robinson in the Royal Society of Arts animate series[19] in 2010. He calls the rise of ADHD 'a modern epidemic', and controversially associated it with the rise of standardised testing in schools: 'Children are besieged with information all day and we wonder why they're distracted.' What they are lacking is any kind of aesthetic experience at school, what they get is the anaesthetic of Ritalin.

In his well-watched TED talk from 2006 – the subject of which we're still talking about now – Sir Ken mentions the example of a young girl called Gillian Lynne who couldn't sit still at school. Gillian went on to become the ballerina and feted choreographer Dame Gillian Lynne, so hardly a failure. He argues

that asking such a person to sit still in a classroom is a waste of her kind of intelligence. 'We need to radically rethink our view of intelligence... We think visually, we think in sound, we think kinaesthetically, we think with our bodies and in abstract.'

Intelligence is dynamic and interactive, not just about rote learning. What people with ADHD will tell you is that they don't have a deficit of attention, they have too much of it, for everything, all the time, all at once.

Impulsivity

The core signs of ADHD are hyperactivity, inattention and impulsiveness, and this diagnosis affects one in 20 children in the UK, though the numbers are higher in the US. The performer and comedian Rory Bremner describes himself growing up as a restless, impetuous and scatty child. Rather than a deficit, he calls it an 'attention surfeit': an over-sensitivity to stimuli. In his adult creative life as a comedian this is endlessly useful, but it made school difficult.

In an interview, Bremner said, 'We try to get children to sit still, to concentrate, to not be distracted and to be organised. For an ordinary child that's difficult, for an ADHD child it's impossible. So they get into trouble and they might be seen as being disruptive, they get sent out of class and each time that happens it takes another little layer of self-esteem, of self-belief, and it wears that child down. The anxiety and the despair will wear them down both in terms of brain development and functionality.'[20]

There is evidence that craft-related learning can help with impulsivity. In his survey of the subject, commissioned by the Ruskin Mill Trust (RMT), Dr Aric Sigman[21] identifies that the process of 'start-to-finish learning' reinforced through a craft-based curriculum cultivates greater sustained attention, self-regulation and deferred gratification that's vital to impulse control.

Ruskin Mill, Gloucestershire is also home to the Field Centre, the research hub for the Ruskin Mill Land Trust and a study centre where staff are trained in their method of Practical Skills Therapeutic Education (PSTE). Matthew Briggs[22] conducted work-based research and a study around the power of craft to help manage impulse-control-related disorders and concluded that crafts were powerful enough to be prescribed to pupils, with specific skills for each individual learning plan, what he calls a 'craft prescription handbook'.

The idea is that the material worked with resists our actions on it and gives feedback, good or bad, as we witness the effect our actions have had. Reflecting on this degree of success enables us to moderate our actions to change the consequences, and 'In turn it builds the basis for reflection as the participant must adjust their will and thinking accordingly in order to meet the desired outcome. Within psychology this process can be seen to stimulate the learner's executive functioning.'

Executive functions of the brain might include inhibitory behaviour, or self-control, cognitive flexibility, the ability to problem-solve and the working memory. Pupils with learning differences often struggle with these, so anything that can help to develop them has to be a good thing.

We have all met people who don't want to try something new, sometimes because they have a misguided vision of the perfection that others will achieve and know that they won't be able to live up to their own expectations. One of the difficulties that students can struggle with is poor self-esteem and a lack of confidence in trying new activities. When trying and feeling that they have failed yet again results in a downward spiral of self-

blame, it can be hard to get them to have another go. The idea of resistant materials is that they become separate from the person and this therefore removes the idea of trying to achieve perfection.

Briggs goes on to say, 'The process of oscillating between good vs bad and positive vs negative effect can lead the learner to see the object as separate from their ego and therefore diminish the attachment of blame. With the disassociation of blame towards their concept of working goal, the learner is free to evaluate the outcome (article) from a third person perspective.' Thus, changing the perspective from personal to outside can remove the notion of personal success or failure, thereby enabling the learner to reflect on the way that they behave.

One of the teachers interviewed by Briggs explained how the 'nature of the craft', with its 'very slow processes', creates the condition in which the learner must react and work; 'the nature of the craft will mean that you have to do it in a certain way, that impulses just don't work. You have to give your own ego away to the ego of the craft.'

Crafts are slow and often repetitive, and this slowing down also enables some time for reflection. There is also evidence that this time enables some inhibitions to develop. Another example cited by Briggs is of a young lad who enjoyed working in the blacksmithing forge, at first in a mindless,

though enthusiastic way. Six months later, he was able to work calmly as if his will itself had been tempered in the fire – a great example of impulse control developed by realising that you can't fight a lump of iron in the forge, you have to work at it. From there he learned not to battle other people, but to work with them.

Executive functions and resistant materials

Executive function is where the brain's prefrontal cortex helps us with short-term memory, monitoring behaviour and regulating impulses; this is the ability to think on our feet and to respond to unexpected events.

This cognitive flexibility is important for problem-solving, something that is as crucial for the workplace as for life situations. Poor executive functioning impairs the ability

to manage emotions, resulting in poor outcomes. Wouldn't it be great if there was an easy solution?

Researchers in Norway have shown[23] that even generalised art education improves behavioural regulation. On the basis that 'Executive functions (EFs) can be conceptualized as a mean of behavioural self-regulation, and difficulties with EFs may adversely affect school success, social function, and cognitive and psychological development'. Over twelve weeks children received creative learning practices from artists in six different artforms (music, drama, dance, poetry, visual arts and photography) delivered for one hour a day, three days a week. Sessions included elements of reflection after each workshop, so learning was absorbed. In their research paper they observe that 'Surprisingly, the intervention group displayed a greater improvement in behavioural regulation with four times as large effect sizes compared to the control group.' Interviews with the teachers showed 'positive effects for the children when it comes to several aspects: collaboration, conflict management, inclusion, vocabulary, and confidence. These factors are regarded as important for EFs development and academic outcome.'

Steiner teachers call this a 'forming of the will', and seen through the lens of Steiner-based education, developing the will, or developing control of will – or executive functions – helps us to control impulsivity, solve problems and respond to change.

Gert Biesta is Professor of Public Education at Maynooth University, Ireland, and at the University of Edinburgh, Scotland, and has written extensively on education and society. Biesta sees the use of resistant materials in education, such as wood, metal and stone, as a demonstration of the dialogue that happens between student, work and self. 'Such work – which can both take place within the context of design education or art education – provides an excellent example of what it means to engage with the experience of resistance (and therefore provides important opportunities for the education of the will), not only because working with such materials can be a frustrating and difficult experience, but also because if one manages to work with such materials in a successful way, one will experience what it means to establish a

dialogical relationship between oneself and what is other – a process in which one will not only find out many things about the materials one is working with, but also about one's own ability to establish and maintain a dialogue, to work through the frustration, to work with the material rather than against it, and so on.'[24]

All of this is well known by Steiner teachers, for whom this is part of their everyday curriculum. In her book *Will Developed Intelligence*, Patricia Livingston writes, 'So much of handwork has to do with waking up, seeing things, and noticing details. Current brain research has found that using the hands opens up neurological pathways that would otherwise atrophy. In other words, the interrelationship of the hand and eye working together allows more neurological pathways to function. So one could say that handwork with young children is a training ground for thinking, and the more one includes the cultivation of beauty and feeling, the more creative will the intellectual thinking become.'[25]

story
Practical Intelligence

When Gavin Pond and Pam Brown decided to team up and open
a community workshop in the small Cotswolds town of Nailsworth,
they named the not-for-profit company they set up to run it
Practical Intelligence – two words that encapsulate everything they
believe about the power of craft.

'Practical intelligence is often neither acknowledged nor respected,'
they state on the website, 'which results in many talented people's
strengths not being recognised or nurtured, and as a consequence
they lose self-confidence. We believe that there is a morality in
craftwork that can inspire confidence and self-belief.'

The two met while they were working at a local Steiner school where
Gavin was teaching craft and Pam was leading the kindergarten.
Both had seen first-hand what craft could do for the children they
taught and wanted to make it available to more people. The
Nailsworth Community Workshop opened in 2009 as a public space
welcoming everyone, regardless of age, ability or income. Today
it is a thriving resource that draws approximately 120 people
to its workshops each week. Those who can pay, do; those who can't,
attend free of charge.

photo: courtesy of Practical Intelligence, Nailsworth

The workshops range from a Maker's Morning where people can just come in and use the tools to make their own stuff, and a Men's Shed (which is open to women but named to appeal to men who are often less good at seeking out social groups), to a thrice-weekly Production Workshop for adults with learning difficulties and a guitar-making project called Pi Guitars. 'Pi started in 2022,' Gavin explains. 'Every Monday and Friday people who are struggling to engage with the world in one way or another – people with mental health issues, or who have lost their job, for example – meet together to build the finest-quality guitars using recycled and locally sourced wood. We then get them sponsored and donate the finished instruments to music charities. Making beautiful things is a big part of what we do here, but it's not the only thing we do. Pi Guitars is about coming together with a shared purpose. Some days everyone is quietly making and other days we talk.'

Pam and Gavin work with children and teenagers too. There are wood, silver and blacksmithing workshops for home-educated eleven- to 18-year-olds and a 'Boys at the Bench' project in which children and young people with complex learning needs and associated social, emotional and behavioural difficulties from a local school come to the workshop to make things.

'The home education children often start with us unable to engage at all,' Pam says, 'then five years later, some of them are able to make a guitar. As well as the practical skills, they have also learned life skills like how to problem-solve and to persevere when things go wrong. It's the same with the Boys from the Bench kids,' Gavin continues. 'Behavioural difficulties are really about a lack of self-regulation – exploding or being totally passive – but when you're engaged in making something you do achieve that middle ground. We usually start off making something the kids can finish in one session, like a key ring, because when they start, a lot of them aren't capable of any kind of delayed gratification. And some of them will spend a whole year having to finish something every time, but slowly we build up, doing a project that takes a week, then

photos: courtesy of Practical Intelligence, Nailsworth

two weeks. They learn to react to the materials and that they can control outcomes by the way they do something. The important thing is to choose the right project – it needs to be one they can take ownership of, even if it's just sanding the edges of a block of wood to put on a key ring, because it feels good to be able to say, "I made that".'

People come to the Nailsworth Community Workshop for many different reasons. Some come to acquire hand skills, others to share the skills they already have, and many come for social contact and a sense of shared endeavour. Jacob and Sam are two regulars. These are their stories:

Jacob

Jacob first came to the Production Workshop on a work scheme with Ruskin Mill College, part of an educational charity, the Ruskin Mill Trust (see page 46), that uses practical land and craft activities to support the development of work and life skills in young people with autism and other learning difficulties. Ten years later, he is at the workshop almost full time and the wooden hangers that he makes have made their way into Royal households.

I did a lot of making at Ruskin Mill. There was plenty of woodwork, as well as the annual coppicing and wood management. Sometimes I would even see a project all the way through from tree to finished object, like a baseball bat. That's part of why I like to work with wood. Going to the Production Workshop was different. It was quite

an industrial space and I learned to work with different woods.
I grew to like it – so much so that even when the work scheme
ended, I still popped in from time to time. Then, when I left
Ruskin Mill, I applied for a joinery course at the local FE college.
But unfortunately, they didn't get enough people to run it and
I had to settle for carpentry. It was only part-time, so I had a chat
with Pam and ended up doing two days here every week too, making
things for them as well as my own stuff on the lathe.

I excelled at carpentry at college, but by the end of the year I'd had
enough. When I heard that the joinery course still wasn't available,
I decided that was me done with education. I had another chat with
Pam and was soon working at the Production Workshop four days
a week. I've been here ever since.

I work mostly on the lathe. It's satisfying when you put the wood
across it and watch it get turned down into a perfect, smaller
cylinder. I like it because when I look at the work I do, I can say that
I made it with my own hands. That's the benefit of handwork, real
achievement – especially when it ends up being given as a Christmas
present by Princess Anne!

Sam

**Sam came to Nailsworth Community Workshop through a local
therapeutic community for drug rehabilitation. A year on, he is one
of the regular volunteers at Pi Guitars.**

Going to the Nailsworth Community Workshop was one of the
volunteering things I was offered as I came towards the end of
the rehabilitation process. It was a way to help re-integrate with
the normal world and engage with something that might get me
back into work. I came to the Men's Shed on a Tuesday afternoon
and it really resonated with me. Coming to this community activity
in a workshop and connecting with people on all sorts of different
paths through the mutual connection of working with our hands
was amazing. As I got to know Gavin, he started talking about
his guitar project. I play the guitar, so I volunteered for that too.

It wasn't something I'd ever done before but I enjoy the creative process of making.

I have always been interested in making. One of my earliest memories as a child is a book I had called *The Way Things Work*. It fascinated me and I was always taking things apart to understand how they functioned. My grandfather was a very practical person – he was a tailor and he also built his own house. I guess I learned a lot of skills from him and then, because of the path my life took, I was often in situations where I had to get myself out of things, and I found I could do that by creating something with my hands. Then, in my late twenties, I also recognised that the process of making things helped with my mental health. I reconnected with that outlet when I came here. Having something practical to do frees your mind to be able to talk about stuff you might not necessarily feel comfortable talking about otherwise.

I come here quite often now, three or four times a week, and I think it will always be a part of my life because it's had such a fundamental effect on me. One of the biggest things is the connection with like-minded people and the sense of joint endeavour. That's not something I have had in my life before.

125

The Craftivist Collective

Sarah Corbett is an award-winning campaigner, author and Ashoka Fellow. In 2009, after a successful career as a professional campaigner for a variety of non-governmental organisations, she founded the Craftivist Collective, a global social enterprise offering projects, tools and events for people interested in trying a quiet, kind and slow form of strategic activism to address social injustice. She calls the methodology behind her approach to craftivism (craft + activism) 'Gentle Protest'. This is her story:

I grew up in an activist family in a low-income area of Liverpool. Our community campaigned on local issues such as social housing, healthcare and jobs, as well as global issues such as fairtrade coffee and the end to South Africa's apartheid. I saw that activism could work if delivered strategically and with kindness to limit polarisation. That experience has shaped me and shaped the way I do activism and craftivism.

The Craftivist Collective came about through my realisation that I was burnt out. As well as my professional activism, I was also a member of several voluntary activist groups in my spare time. I didn't feel I fitted in – I am an introvert, I don't like conflict, and I do enjoy fashion. I also doubted the effectiveness of many of our protest actions and questioned some of the motives. The big question facing me – and which I kept avoiding because it sent me into a downward spiral – was whether, given all that, I could go on being an activist.

A few days before making a long train journey from London to Glasgow for work, I spotted a small cross-stitch kit in a local boutique. I struggle to write and work on trains because I get travel sick, so when I saw this simple, affordable craft kit I bought it on impulse to pass the time in a creative way.

Sarah Corbett

Sarah Corbett photo: Craftivist Collective, Liz Seabrook

As I got started, my hands separating the thread were shaky and I was impatient with the needle. These were visible signs of how stressed I was, something I had not acknowledged before. After a while, the repetitive hand actions helped to steady my breathing and I became calmer. Then an elderly couple sitting opposite me asked me what I was doing. Talking to strangers isn't something British people do very often, so the fact that they had initiated a conversation intrigued me. Was it because I was making something? And was the smallness of what I was making part of the appeal? Because I am an activist geek, I immediately thought that if I'd been cross-stitching a quote about inequality or another issue, rather than a teddy, it could have been a natural opportunity to start an important conversation in a gentle way.

So, the first seeds were sown. I carried on cross-stitching and found that the process of using my hands in this repetitive way continued to be calming. It also felt empowering to see that I was physically creating something from start to finish. The process helped me with my critical thinking too, connecting my head, hands and heart together so I could use the comfort of craft to ask myself big and often uncomfortable questions such as, 'Is the activism I am

Malala Yousafzai joining in at an event photo: Craftivist Collective

currently doing strategic or reactive? Is there a bit of ego in there? If I was a politician, how would I respond to these protests?'

My gut feeling was that the process of repetitive, small handicrafts could be a useful tool to add to the activism toolkit. Not to replace other forms of activism but to enhance critical thinking, help with preventing activist burnout and attract audiences nervous of traditional and more extrovert forms of activism. So, in the summer of 2008, I googled 'Craft and Activism' and the word 'craftivism', coined by Betsy Greer in 2003, popped up.

There were no craftivism projects or groups I was able to join in with in the UK, so, with Betsy's permission, I began creating my own projects. My first was making cross-stitched 'Mini Protest Banners': postcard-sized tapestries of quotes or questions about injustice that I would hang in places relevant to the issue, such as shopping centres or financial districts. I also stitched a handkerchief as a bespoke gift for my local Member of Parliament. Her office staff had told me that contacting them with petitions was a waste of our time and any charity's money, and I wanted to build a relationship with her as a concerned constituent and critical friend, rather than as an aggressive activist.

This is what I hand-stitched:

Dear MP,

As my MP I am asking you to please use your powerful position to challenge injustices, change structures that are keeping people poor and fight for a more just and fairer world. I know being an MP is a tough and big job but please DON'T BLOW IT, this is your chance to make a real positive difference. ☺
Yours in hope,
Sarah

The MP and her staff responded very warmly to my handkerchief gift and I developed a positive relationship with them, working on issues we agreed on and listening to each other better where we differed. Before long, other people around the world began to contact me wanting to join in my projects so, in January 2009, I founded the Craftivist Collective.

One of our most well-known campaigns is one that I was asked to create for ShareAction, to encourage a large and much-loved British retail company to pay their staff the real Living Wage. A group of Craftivists, each carefully selected because they fitted the company's customer demographic, hand-stitched bespoke messages onto 24 handkerchiefs as gifts for the 14 board members, five Chief Investment Officers of its largest shareholder companies and five celebrity models from their recent advertising campaign. The stitched messages encouraged them not to 'blow it' but to use their power for good governance and lead the way in the retail sector. Fourteen of the hankies were respectfully delivered to the board during the company's 2015 AGM, asking the CEO for a meeting to discuss becoming a Living Wage employer. The campaign worked. In April 2016, following a series of meetings and gifts in the shape of handmade Christmas and Valentine's Day cards, they announced they would increase the pay of 50,000 employees from minimum wage to be in line with the UK National Living Wage.

Mini-scrolls campaign
photo: Craftivist Collective

I create campaigns for different charities and campaign groups, as well as for creative organisations such as Secret Cinema and the Victoria & Albert Museum. I created a project supporting Fashion Revolution, protesting the ugly side of the fashion industry with Mini Fashion Statements. These were small paper scrolls containing handwritten questions about the story behind items of clothing – such as poor conditions for workers, or the use of materials that are damaging to the environment – which we tied with pretty ribbon, added a handwritten invitation to 'please read me' and dropped into the pockets of garments in fashion stores around the world. I called it 'shop dropping' rather than shop lifting. The project was covered on the homepage of the BBC News website.

These projects are deliberately non-confrontational and strategically focused forms of activism/craftivism. I call our

Flow

'The best moments in our lives are not the passive, receptive, relaxing times... The best moments usually occur if a person's body or mind is stretched to its limits in a voluntary effort to accomplish something difficult and worthwhile.'
Mihaly Csikszentmihalyi[26]

The Hungarian-American psychologist Mihaly Csikszentmihalyi recognised and named the psychological concept of flow, a highly focused mental state when we are completely absorbed in what we are doing, and able to ignore everything else. Flow is an elusive state, much like falling asleep, that when longed-for is hard to achieve. Rather, it comes upon us when we are engrossed,

so when we least expect it. Csikszentmihalyi felt that we need an increasing degree of skill and commitment to keep us engaged – something neither too hard, nor too easy – writing in his book, *Flow: The Psychology of Happiness*, 'Enjoyment appears at the boundary between boredom and anxiety, when the challenges are just balanced with the person's capacity to act.'[27] So, if you are a good knitter, a little stocking stitch won't engage you but some testing lace might be frustrating, so perhaps a Fair Isle pattern might hit the Goldilocks moment somewhere in the middle. The late Sir Ken Robinson, author and Professor of Arts Education, called it finding your 'element'.[28] It must be active and you must be in control.

approach to craftivism Gentle Protest, because I want to make clear what we *don't do*. When people think of activism, they often think of confrontation and aggression. Gentle Protest, in contrast, is about careful campaign strategies focused on compassion for others and for ourselves. It's about empathy with people affected by unfairness as well as with powerholders, channelling our anger and sadness at injustice into beautiful physical catalysts for thought, conversation and change. I try to create thoughtful projects that support people to be kind, courageous and effective citizens.

Sadly, it's important to state that not all craftivism is gentle nor effective. Some of it focuses on personality not policy, some is too vague. You could cross-stitch 'Stop the War' and gain many likes on Instagram, yet if it's not clear which war you are talking about and there are no practical steps to bring about peace, it's not empowering.

Once the attention is fully directed we lose our self-consciousness and may have less experience of recurring negative thoughts running through our heads, or the resultant anxiety it brings.

Having the right craft is also important, Robinson believes. 'The extent to which we find our jobs or hobbies enjoyable is the extent to which there is a match between our sensorimotor, cognitive, psychological and interpersonal characteristic, our social and cultural orientation and the characteristics (realistically and symbolically) of the job or hobby. It is this congruence, this match of person characteristics and activity characteristics, that triggers and sustains intrinsic motivation.'

The motivation comes from the chemistry, or flow, between person and activity and the output reflects that, though it's not always the final product that is the motivation. In *Activities: Reality and Symbol*, Fidler and Velde write, 'This process involves a holistic experience in which kinaesthetic demands merge with aesthetic demands… The opportunity to produce a material good where there was none before often results in self-fulfilment… Crafts achieve elements of language when the product becomes an expression of emotions, desires and ideals visible to self and others.'[29]

My background in activism means that I'm pragmatic about how we can make a difference. Martin Luther King Jr said that activists need 'a tough mind and a tender heart'. I have this tattooed on my shoulder because activism or craftivism is heart work and therefore hard work if we try to do it effectively.

It is important that gentle craftivism is seen as just one tool in the activism toolkit, not to replace other forms of activism or to fix an injustice on its own but as part of a larger movement for positive change. We need to look at craftivism as if we're designers crafting something to help solve a problem or answer a need. That means being clear about what issues we care about, what the reasons are for the injustice, who are the largest powerholders, how best to engage them in their decision-making and where craftivism can be useful to address it. In some situations craftivism is not the best tool to use.

The process of handicrafts can be powerful for activism: once your hands are used in the comforting repetitive action of hand-stitching, your mind can then engage in critical thinking about your campaign strategy and you can be mindful of what you are bringing to your craft: is there a little bit of ego or some presumptions you need to unpick? For all my projects and workshops I create 'crafterthought' questions for craftivists to reflect on while we're using our hands. Challenging questions such as 'What are my values and am I threading them through what I do, say and think before I tell other people what to do?' And 'How would I feel if I were to receive this object? Would I feel patronised or demonised or would I feel genuinely accountable and encouraged?' The aim is to put ourselves in the shoes of people we might distrust or whose policies we dislike, to challenge our own values so that we practise what we preach and to be in solidarity not sympathy with those directly affected by harmful systems, structures, behaviours or cultures.

The spiritual part in me believes that there is a magical energy in the objects that we create, therefore if we take time to make something with a clear mind, and a strategic plan, in hope and with loving intentions, then the person receiving it will feel that. As one part of the activist jigsaw, gentle craftivism can be useful, effective and empowering in helping to make our world a healthier, happier, more harmonious place for all, full of kind and active citizens working together for societal good.

A class in sloyd, 1899 photo: Frances Benjamin Johnston, 1899 (Library of Congress)

The influence of sloyd

Sloyd or *slöjd* (see page 36), is a system of handicraft-based education that is still taught as a compulsory subject in Finnish, Danish, Swedish and Norwegian schools, although its influence has been felt around the world, particularly in North America.

In 1875, Otto Salomon opened a sloyd school in Nääs, alongside a training centre for sloyd teachers that had ripples throughout Scandinavia and on to the United States, Germany, Mexico, Japan and England. By 1917 over 6,000 teachers had been trained there, and through these teachers and his handbook for teachers and the transcripts of his lectures, his ideas spread.

Gustav Larsson trained at Nääs, and supported by the Swiss philanthropist and reformer Pauline Agassiz Shaw, he went on to become principal of the North Bennet Street Industrial School, in Boston, which also became the Sloyd Training School of Boston. He wrote his own training manual in 1902, adjusting Salomon's curriculum to the needs of the local population, and also edited *The Sloyd Record*, a regular school newsletter, from 1904 to 1912. The purpose of his writing was clear from the foreword:
'*Unfortunately, sloyd has often been superficially judged from its outward symbols only, while the vital principles for which it stands have been overlooked. It is hoped that this little publication may help to convince teachers and other promoters of education that the principles of sloyd are broad and universal, and that as an effective educational agent it deserves a place in our schools.'*[1]

And later he went on, '*Most of the exponents of the various systems of manual training agree that education is the end to be obtained, but they differ as to the meaning of the word "education". Some think that it refers only to a training for purely mental development, while others think it refers to a training for the sake of getting a livelihood. Most progressive thinkers and writers upon the subject, however, claim that the hand should be employed, as a tool of the brain, to supplement prevailing methods and to develop general power.'*[2]

Larsson was quite forward-thinking in his outlook and went on to influence art education in the US. Over 100 years later, the education at the North Bennet Street School is still based on the sloyd principles and a 'life in craft'.[3]

Other students of the Nääs training school were Meri Toppelius, who went to teach sloyd in Chicago, and Ednah Rich, who became principal of the State Normal School of Manual Arts and Home Economics in Santa Barbara. Despite women being respected as influential teachers, the students were still regimented into activities deemed suitable for their gender; that is, there were not many girls in the wood workshop. Rich's book *Paper Sloyd*,[4] created templates, or *models*, for younger children in preparation for their transition to either wood sloyd or sewing and cooking (for the girls). The models range from simple fan

185

Plate VIII. Position: Smoothing, &c., with the spokeshave.

Standing position for smoothing with the spokeshave

from *The Teacher's Hand-book of Slöjd*, Otto Salomon, 1892

concertinas and pin wheels for the first year, to more complex origami-style hexagonal trays and a whisk-broom holder (a hand-held brush or broom). In her book, Rich wrote of the benefits of working with paper:

'*Observation is quickened; eyes are trained to see right lines and distances, thus aiding in free-hand drawing and writing; while the hand and wrist muscles, being used for a definite purpose, unconsciously become obedient assistants. Paper Sloyd rightly presented justifies itself.*'[5]

Another student of sloyd was Ella Victoria Dobbs, who had been taught at the Throop Polytechnic Institute in Pasadena – now the California Institute of Technology – who graduated in 1900 and then became a faculty member. Later in her career, as Assistant Professor of Manual Arts, University of Missouri, she developed a methodology to combine the arts and handwork in the curriculum with several publications: *Illustrative Handwork for Elementary Schools, A Desk Manual for Classroom Teachers* (1917), *Primary Handwork* (1922) and *First Steps in Weaving* (1938).

Introducing her theory, Dobbs writes about the newness of handwork and how it is often classed as a special subject, separate and set apart from the other subjects on the curriculum. She argued for more integration: '*We have begun to realise that handwork is valuable not only for its product in things made but also for the effect upon the maker; that it is not only a subject to be studied for its own sake, but may be a helpful method of styling other subjects; that it is not only an end in itself, but that it is also a means to an end.*'[6] Dobbs proposed a freer and more expressive form of expression, '*free in its methods and without emphasis upon technical processes*', more akin to the art room than the workshop.

In her *Illustrative Handwork* manual, Dobbs advocated making posters, dioramas and models that allowed self-expression, while supporting other subjects, such as history and geography, to encompass the learning styles of different pupils, using it as a teaching method rather than as a subject, what she called 'educative handwork'. She explained, 'Handwork for the sake of the thing to be made is one thing. Handwork for the sake of being able to make, i.e. skill, is another. Handwork for the sake of the personal effect upon the worker is still another, and is always important, if not the most important.'[7]

The sloyd pedagogy as developed by Salomon is a holistic craft process that includes design and problem solving, not just a mechanical process. The emphasis is on self-development, so rather than simply a system for learning woodwork, it focuses on personal development of the individual. The Industrial Revolution of the nineteenth century increased the pressure on educators to teach the skills that employers needed and to prepare citizens for real life. Salomon was keen to point out that while educational sloyd helped pupils to develop

FIG. 22.—Sloyd knife, No. 7.

A typical sloyd knife, from *Educational Woodworking for Home and School*, Joseph Charles Park 1912

themselves, it was not a scheme to produce working craftspeople; *'What, then, is the aim of educational slöjd? To utilise… the educative force which lies in rightly directed bodily labour, as a means of developing in the pupils physical and mental powers which will be a sure and evident gain to them for life.'*[8]

Salomon also recognised that there was class prejudice against this less literary, manual work. *'Respect for manual labor! Yes. Who does not in our day entertain at least a theoretical respect for manual labor and for the labourer himself; yet, be it incidentally remarked, less for them as individuals, than as members of the whole class, that in and with the labor unions begins to conquer for itself a certain significance, and consequently must, with other factors, be taken into account. But how is it, then, in reality, with this "respect"? How many fathers of the more educated class allow their sons, without its being positively necessary, to become mechanics, or to devote themselves otherwise to manual work? And is there not to be found among the labourers themselves the wish that their children may become something "better", that is, be reckoned as belonging to another class?'*[9]

Benjamin Hoffman also noted: *'We no longer absolutely despise hard bodily labor as we did a century ago, when to do nothing was considered more honourable than to work; yet even today we attach a certain stigma of inferiority to all forms of bodily labour. In the social world, the clerk ranks higher than the skilled artisan and the workmen themselves are only too apt to consider that their labour is less honourable than that of their masters. This perverted idea may be a survival of the opinion that prevailed in the Middle Ages, when all rough work was done by serfs.'*[10] Yet despite these protestations, rough and inferior kinds of labour were referenced in his handbook.

Although there were an estimated 12 different branches of sloyd, Salomon advocated sticking to one branch, so as not to overtax the teachers, settling on woodwork, with which sloyd is now associated. He devised a list of criteria by which each branch should be measured – including straw plaiting, brush making, basket making and cardboard work – and deemed that only carpentry met with all of them.

The handbook for teachers outlines the aims of sloyd instruction:[11]

Attendance at slöjd instruction should be voluntary on the part of the pupils. In order to ensure this the work must fulfil the following conditions:

1 It must be useful.
2 It must not require fatiguing preparatory exercises in the use of the various tools.
3 It must afford variety.
4 It must be capable of being carried out by the pupils themselves.
5 It must be real work, not play.
6 It must not be so-called knick-knacks – that is, articles of luxury.
7 It must become the property of the pupil.
8 It must correspond with the capabilities of the pupils.
9 It must be of such a nature that it can be completed with exactness.
10 It must admit neatness and cleanliness.
11 It must exercise the thinking powers and not be purely mechanical.
12 It must strengthen and develop the bodily powers.
13 It must assist in developing the sense of form.
14 It must allow the use of numerous manipulations and various tools.

Decorative work for its own ends was thought a bad idea, as it might encourage the use of decoration to conceal poor workmanship and 'throw dust in the eyes of others'. Working by artificial light was also to be avoided, and plans were laid out in the teacher's handbook to describe how a classroom should be set out to make the best use of space.

As with many practical classes, carving out space within the timetable to have a long-enough lesson period is a problem – crafts are time and space hungry. Otto Salomon recommends four hours a week to be spent on sloyd classes, 'though six hours would be better.' He continues, 'A *slöjd* lesson ought not to last less than an hour and a half, or more than two hours and a half. It ought, if possible, to intervene between hours devoted to intellectual instruction, because it offers a wholesome variety for mind and body.'

The educational argument for visual learning can also be co-opted by the economic argument for 'useful' vocational training. Hoffman was Superintendent of the Baron de Hirsch Fund Trade Schools, as the system was already being used for training up carpenters, rather than as a general system of education, so the distinction comes between 'manual' education and technical or industrial training. Hoffman believed, *'The sloyd has for its first object to give an indirect preparation for life by teaching branches of certain trades and by imparting a general dexterity to the hand – to train the hand as the obedient servant of the brain… It embraces the doctrine which educators and teachers have been preaching for a long time – that of giving a practical direction to mental activity. Man is not only born to think, but also to do. He is a creative animal; he can and must embody his ideas in form.'*[12]

Further reading

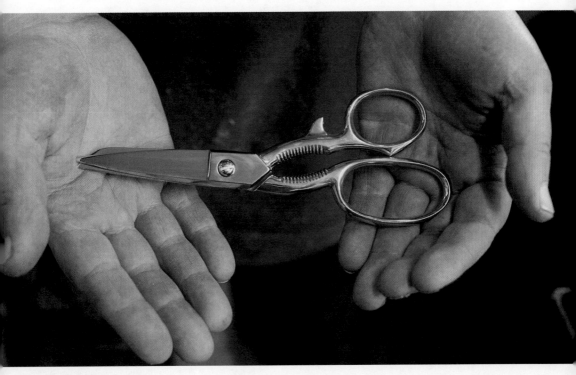

Ernest Wright photo: Carmel King

Adamson, G. (Ed.) *The Craft Reader* (New York: Berg Publishers, 2010)

Briggs, Matthew, Benefits of craft for impulse control related disorders, MSc thesis, (Crossfields Institute, 2014)

Cavalli, Alberto, *The Master's Touch: Essential Elements of Artisanal Excellence*, originally published in Italy in 2014 as *Il valore del mestiere*, Michelangelo Foundation

Corbett, Sarah, *Craftivist Collective Handbook* (unbound 2023)

Corkhill, Betsan, *Knitting for Health and Wellness: Knit yourself a flexible mind* (Flat Bear Publishing, 2014)

Crafts Council, Craft Club: A National Campaign for Craft, Annual report 2018–19, published 2019

Crafts Council, Studying Craft 16: trends in craft education and training, Dr Emma Pooley and Andrew Rowell, October 2016

Crawford, Matthew, *The Case for Working with Your Hands: Or Why Office Work is Bad for Us and Fixing Things Feels Good* (Penguin, 2010)

Creative and Cultural Activities and Wellbeing in Later Life, April 2018, Age UK

Creative Health, APPG on Arts Health and Wellbeing, July 2017

Csikszentmihalyi, Mihaly, *Flow: The Psychology of Happiness* (Rider, 1992)

Evetts, Cynthia and Peloquin, Suzanne, *Mindful Crafts as Therapy: Engaging More Than Hands* (F.A. Davis, 2017)

References

Part One
Mind + Body

Fancourt, Daisy, and Steptoe, Andrew, Effects of creativity on social and behavioral adjustment in 7- to 11-year-old children (UCL, 2018)

Gardner, H., *Frames of Mind: The Theory of Multiple Intelligences* (Basic Books, 1983)

Gauntlett, David, *Making is Connecting: The Social Meaning of Creativity, from DIY and Knitting to YouTube and Web 2.0* (Polity Press, 2011)

Hanscom, Angela, *Balanced and Barefoot: How Unrestricted Outdoor Play Makes for Strong, Confident, and Capable Children* (New Harbinger Press, 2016)

Leader, Darian, *Hands: What We Do With Them – and Why* (Hamish Hamilton, 2016)

Magsamen, Susan and Ross, Ivy, *Your Brain on Art: How the Arts Transform Us* (Canongate Books, 2023)

Matthews, Rachael, *The Mindfulness in Knitting* (Leaping Hare Press, 2017)

Pollanen, S. (2011), Beyond Craft and Art: A pedagogical model for craft as self-expression, International Journal of Education Through Art. 7. 111–125. 10.1386/eta.7.2.111_1

Robertson, Seonaid M., *Creative Crafts in Education* (Routledge, 1952)

Robinson, Ken, *The Element: How finding your passion changes everything* (Penguin, 2010)

Ruskin, John, *Stones of Venice*, Vol 2, Ch VI, from The Nature of Gothic (1851–3)

Power of Making (V&A Publishing, 2011)

Sigman, Aric Dr, Practically Minded: The Benefits and Mechanisms Associated with a Craft-Based Curriculum (Ruskin Mill Educational Trust, 2008)

Whittaker, David J., *The Impact and Legacy of Educational Sloyd: Head and hands in harness* (Routledge, 2014)

Winnicott, Donald, *Playing and Reality* (Routledge, 1971)

Yair, Karen Dr, Craft and Wellbeing, Crafts Council, 2011

1 Stout D., Chaminade T., 'Stone tools, language and the brain in human evolution.' *Philos Trans R Soc Lond B Biol Sci.* 2012;367(1585):75–87. doi:10.1098/rstb.2011.0099

2 Uomini N.T., Meyer G.F., 'Shared Brain Lateralization Patterns in Language and Acheulean Stone Tool Production: A Functional Transcranial Doppler Ultrasound Study' (2013), PLoS ONE 8(8): e72693. https://doi.org/10.1371/journal.pone.0072693

3 Engels, Friedrich, *Dialectics of Nature* (1883), ch IX. 'Before the first flint could be fashioned into a knife by human hands, a period of time must probably have elapsed in comparison with which the historical period known to us appears insignificant. But the decisive step was taken: *the hand became free* and could henceforth attain ever greater dexterity and skill, and the greater flexibility thus acquired was inherited and increased from generation to generation. Thus the hand is not only the organ of labour, *it is also the product of labour.*'

4 Groth, Camilla. 'Design and Craft Thinking Analysed as Embodied Cognition' (2016) FORMakademisk. 9. 1–21. 10.7577/formakademisk.1481

5 Ruskin, John, *Stones of Venice*, Vol 2, Ch VI, from The Nature of Gothic (1851–3)

6 Magsamen, Susan and Ross, Ivy, *Your Brain on Art: How the Arts Transform Us* (Canongate Books, 2023)

7 Bernstein, N. A., The Co-ordination and Regulation of Movements (Transl. 1967)

8 Wood, Nicola, 'The new journeyman: The role of an expert learner in eliciting and transmitting skilled knowledge', Sheffield Hallam University Research Archive (SHURA); http://shura.shu.ac.uk/505/

9 Bill Lucas, co-founder of the Centre of Real-World Learning (CRL) at Winchester University and the Expansive Education Network, speaking at Making Matters at the Royal Society of Arts, 2017. https://www.thersa.org/events/2017/07/making-matters

10 Groth, Camilla, 'Design and Craft Thinking Analysed as Embodied Cognition', University of South-Eastern Norway, June 2016; DOI: 10.7577/formakademisk.1481

11 Lewis, C. S., 'Good Work and Good Works', from *The World's Last Night and Other Essays*, Harcourt Brace (Edition 1960)

12 Cavalli, Alberto, *The Master's Touch: Essential Elements of Artisanal Excellence*, originally published in Italy in 2014 as *Il valore del mestiere* by the Michelangelo Foundation

Part Two
Education + Learning

1 (Isaacson, Walter (2007), *Einstein: His Life and Universe*, New York, NY: Simon & Schuster.)

2 The Organisation for Economic Co-operation and Development (OECD) report, 2018, oecd.org, accessed June 2020

3 Eyestone, June E., 'The Influence of Swedish Sloyd and Its Interpreters on American Art Education.' *Studies in Art Education* 34, no. 1 (1992): 28-38. Accessed January 29, 2021. doi:10.2307/1320596

4 Salomon, Otto, *The Teacher's Handbook of slöjd: as practised and taught at Nääs, containing explanations and details of each exercise* (Silver Burdett & Co., 1892)

5 ibid.

6 Barter, S, 'Manual instruction; woodwork; (the English sloyd)', https://archive.org/details/manualinstructio00bartrich/page/10/mode/2up

7 Dewey, John, *Democracy and Education: An Introduction to the Philosophy of Education* (1916) Copyright © 2001 The Pennsylvania State University

8 Ibid.

9 Graves, Bernard, *The Waldorf Handwork and Craft Curriculum*

10 Notes for a lecture in Bristol, 1943, www.karlkoniginstitute.org

11 Gardner, H., *Frames of Mind: The Theory of Multiple Intelligences* (Basic Books, 1983)

12 Eisner, E., *The Arts and the Creation of Mind* (Yale University Press, 2002)

13 Seton, Ernest Thompson, *The Birch-bark Roll of the Woodcraft Indians, containing their constitution, laws, games, and deeds* (Doubleday, Page & Company, 1907)

14 *Our Roots: The Story of the Forest School 1929–1940*, published by Forest School Camps, www.fsc.org.uk

15 https://forestschoolassociation.org/

16 https://www.lotc.org.uk

17 *Refining the Vessel: Practical Skills Therapeutic Education: a fourfold approach*, RMT book series, https://www.thefieldcentre.org.uk/publications

18 'What are the Therapeutic and Pedagogical Benefits of Craft for Impulse Control related Disorders within the SEN Further Education Sector', Matt Briggs, MsC, 2014.

19 'Practically Minded' (2019), https://www.thefieldcentre.org.uk/papers-and-reports

20 National statistics, DCMS Economic Estimates 2019 (provisional): Gross Value Added, DCMS 2021accessed www.gov.uk, Feb 2021

21 Creative subjects being squeezed, schools tell BBC, Published 30 January 2018, education- 42862996 BBC survey

22 Crafts Council research, 'Studying Craft 16: trends in craft education and training', October 2016, Dr Emma Pooley and Andrew Rowell

23 https://www.culturallearningalliance.org.uk/policy-and-practice-round-up-april-2023/

24 Kneebone, Roger, *Expert: Understanding the path to mastery*, 2021, Penguin Books

25 Strategy 2020_2030 Arts Council England.pdf

26 Fancourt_et_al-2018-Annals_of_the_New_York_Academy_of_Sciences.pdf

27 See, Huat Beng and Kokotsaki, Dimitra, 'Impact of arts education on the cognitive and non-cognitive outcomes of school-aged children: A review of evidence', Durham University https://www.artscouncil.org.uk/durham-commission-creativity-and-education

29 Gardner, H., *Frames of Mind: The Theory of Multiple Intelligences* (Basic Books, 1983)

30 Article at www.royalacademy.org.uk, 20 July 2020

31 https://www.economist.com/business/2014/01/04/the-art-and-craft-of-business

32 https://www.thersa.org/globalassets/pdfs/reports/rsaj3881_ours_to_master_report_11.15_web.pdf

33 *Making Matters*, RSA, 4 July 2017; Funded and invited by Comino Foundation

34 Ibid.

35 Walter Gropius in a speech on the Bauhaus ahead of the Stuttgart Building Exhibition, 1924

36 Itten, Johannes, *Design and form: the basic course at the Bauhaus and later*

37 Manifesto of the Bauhaus (Weimar, 1919) sourced from Adamson, Glenn (Ed.) *The Craft Reader* (Bloomsbury, 2010)

38 First published in *Crafting Textiles in a Digital Age*, Nithikul Nimkulrat (Ed.) (Bloomsbury Academic, 2016)

39 Quoted by Eleanor Duckworth, student and interpreter to Piaget, *Piaget rediscovered*, The Arithmetic Teacher, Vol. 11, No. 7 (November 1964)

Part Three
Well-being + Activism

1 Evetts, Cynthia and Peloquin, Suzanne, *Mindful Crafts as Therapy: Engaging More Than Hands*, (F. A. Davis Company, 2017)

2 Fidler, Gail and Velde, Beth, *Activities: Reality and Symbol* (Slack Inc., 1999)

3 Stuart, Denis, *Dear Duchess: Millicent, Duchess of Sutherland, 1867–1955* (Victor Gollancz, 1982)

4 https://finecellwork.co.uk/blogs/blog-events/open-the-gates-the-story-so-far

5 Dissanayake, Ellen, 'The Pleasure and Meaning of Making', 1995, American Craft 55(2): 40–45

6 Dr Fiona Hackney, Hannah Maughan and Sarah Desmarais, *Journal of Textile Design Research and Practice* Volume 4, Issue 1, pp 33–62 DOI: 10.1080/20511787.2016.1256139; https://cocreatingcare.wordpress.com

7 https://www.gov.uk/government/speeches/the-power-of-the-arts-and-social-activities-to- improve-the-nations-health? 20July, 2018

8 Bone, J.K. and Fancourt, D. 'Arts, Culture & the Brain: A literature review and new epidemiological analyses'. London: Arts Council England (2022)

9 https://www.pointsoflight.gov.uk/handmade-for-dementia

10 HUG™ has been evaluated with people living with dementia as part of Welsh Government-funded LAUGH EMPOWERED research. The study, which took place in a residential care home over six months, found that HUG™ can make a significant improvement to the wellbeing of people living with dementia by reducing anxiety, improving posture and stimulating communication. It has also been found to improve cognitive and functional ability in some people living with dementia who have used HUG™ for six months (Treadaway, Pool and Johnson 2020)

11 Albers, Anni, *On Weaving*, Wesleyan University Press (1965)

12 Winnicott, Donald, *Playing and Reality* (Routledge, 1971)

13 Leader, Darian, *Hands: What We Do With Them – and Why* (Hamish Hamilton, 2016)

14 Hanscom, Angela, *Balanced and Barefoot: How Unrestricted Outdoor Play Makes for Strong, Confident, and Capable Children* (New Harbinger Press, 2016)

15 Musall, S., Kaufman, M. T., Juavinett, A. L. *et al.* 'Single-trial neural dynamics are dominated by richly varied movements. 'Nat Neurosci 22, 1677–1686 (2019). https://doi.org/10.1038/s41593-019- 0502-4

16 Ibid.

17 http://www.freud.org.uk

18 Baird B., Smallwood J., Mrazek M. D., Kam J. W., Franklin

Appendix

M.S., Schooler J.W. 'Inspired by distraction: mind wandering facilitates creative incubation.' *Psychological Science*. 2012 Oct 1; 23(10):1117–22. doi: 10.1177/0956797612446024. Epub 2012 Aug 31. PMID: 22941876

19 Robinson, Ken, 'Changing Education Paradigms' talk for RSA animate 2010, https://www.thersa.org/discover/videos/rsa-animate/2010/10/rsa-animate---changing- paradigms

20 Rory Bremner On Living With ADHD, *Lorraine*, Nov 13, 2014, https://youtu.be/OiKs5ADJcAg

21 Sigman, Dr Aric, 'Practically Minded: The Benefits and Mechanisms Associated with a Craft - Based Curriculum', 2008

22 'What are the Therapeutic and Pedagogical Benefits of Craft for Impulse Control related Disorders within the SEN Further Education Sector?', Matthew Briggs, Msc in Practical Skills Therapeutic Education

23 Andersen, P. N., Klausen, M. E. and Skogli E. W., 'Art of Learning – An Art-Based Intervention Aimed at Improving Children's Executive Functions'. *Frontiers in Psychology* (2019) 10:1769. doi: 10.3389/fpsyg.2019.01769

24 Biesta, Gert, 'The Educational Significance of the Experience of Resistance: Schooling and the Dialogue between Child and World', University of Stirling, UK, p98. *Other Education: The Journal of Educational Alternatives* ISSN 2049–2162, Volume 1 (2012), Issue 1 pp. 92–103.

25 Mitchell, David, and Livingston, Patricia, *Will Developed Intelligence: The Handwork and Practical Arts*, revised edition (Waldorf Publications, 2016)

26 Csikszentmihalyi, Mihaly, *Flow: The Psychology of Happiness* (1992)

27 Ibid.

28 Robinson, Ken, *The Element: How finding your passion changes everything*, (Penguin 2010)

29 Fidler, Gail and Velde, Beth, *Activities: Reality and Symbol* (Slack Inc., 1999)

1 Gustav Larsson, *Sloyd*, 1902

2 Ibid.

3 North Bennet Street School website https://www.nbss.edu

4 Rich, Ednah Anne, Paper *Sloyd: A Handbook for Primary Grades*, Ginn & Company (1905)

5 Ibid.

6 Dobbs, Ella Victoria, *Illustrative Handwork for Elementary School Subjects, a Desk Manual for Classroom Teachers* (Macmillan New York, 1917)

7 Dobbs, Ella Victoria, *Illustrative handwork for elementary school subjects, a desk manual for classroom teachers* (Macmillan New York, 1917), p13

8 *The Teacher's Hand-Book of Slöjd: as Practised and Taught at Nääs*, By Otto Salomon, containing explanations and details of each exercise, English edition (George Philip & Son, London, 1891), accessed Jan 2021 via googlebooks

9 Salomon, Otto Aron, Murray Butler, Nicholas, Carpenter, William Henry, *The Slöjd in the Service of the School* (Industrial Education Association, 1888), accessed Google Books, Jan 2021

10 Hoffman, B. B., Salomon, O. Aron. *The Sloyd system of wood working: with a brief description of the Eva Rodhe model series and an historical sketch of the growth of the manual training idea.* (New York: American Book Company, 1892) accessed archive.org, Jan 2021

11 Salomon, Otto Aron, Murray Butler, Nicholas, Carpenter, William Henry, *The Slöjd in the Service of the School* (Industrial Education Association, 1888), accessed Google Books, Jan 2021

12 Hoffman, B. B., Salomon, O. Aron. *The Sloyd system of wood working: with a brief description of the Eva Rodhe model series and an historical sketch of the growth of the manual training idea.* (New York: American book company, 1892) accessed archive.org, Jan 2021

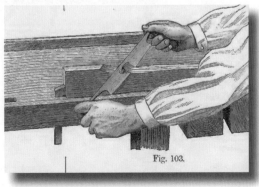

Woodwork exercise

from *The Teacher's Hand-book of Slöjd*, Otto Salomon, 1892.

Fig. 103.

Cleo Mussi Mosaics photo: Carmel King

Q
QUICKTHORN